CW00705568

Beyond

Beyond

Dialogues About Aware Beingness

Jan Kersschot

Text, quotes, design and cover photograph by Jan Kersschot

Copyright Jan Kersschot 2018

I would like to express my gratitude to all who have contributed to these dialogues. This book contains transcripts of dialogues and interviews about nondualism in Belgium, Holland, Spain and Japan.

I frequently reordered and edited the questions and answers for optimal flow, readability, and impact - except for chapter 4 "Passionate about Nondualism" which was copied without any editing from the interview by Patrick Kicken from Holland. The link to the full interview is available on www.kersschot.com

Disclaimer

The author and publisher disclaim responsibility for any adverse effects of any kind resulting directly or indirectly from information contained in this book.

Nondualism is rather about
seeing than labeling.
It is rather about
being than becoming.
It is rather about
us than about me.

The conversations in this book
are not dialogues but monologues.

Contents

Nondualism points to
the single undivided field
which doesn't exclude anyone.
That spaciousness is what we are.

Introduction

Isn't it amazing that we are? Just to *be*. And isn't it stunning that we are also *aware* that we are? This combination of being and the 'awareness of being' could be described as 'aware beingness.' This aware beingness is never elsewhere, it is never fading. It is reading these very words right now.

However, we will not be able to describe this aware beingness. But what can happen is that all the misconceptions about who or what we really are, are unmasked. And yet, nobody is *doing* this unmasking. Even the sense of individuality is something which is witnessed by awareness. So, it is not you or me 'doing' the witnessing, it is an *impersonal* witnessing. A person can never attain access to this.

This 'beingness' witnesses our environment, our bodily sensations, our thoughts and our feelings. And this is also true for the other people. It is the same aware beingness. Isn't that amazing? It is one single awareness witnessing all these stories. It is the spaciousness in which everything and everyone can arise. It is the light within the images in our own story, and in billions of other movies. In that sense, one can say there is no division.

This aware beingness is and perceives everyone and everything effortlessly, without being separate from what it perceives. In other words, there is no separation between the aware space and ourselves. It is all one substance. It is not at a distance from us. And nobody is excluded from this space. This aware beingness is what *we all are*.

Jan Kersschot
January 2018

What is everywhere
and cannot be reached?
What sees everything
but cannot be seen?

Nondualism

Q: Where do you start from when talking about nondualism?

JK: Nobody can say, 'I am not.' To say this, one needs to *be* first. This sense of 'I am' is true for everyone. It is so simple and so available without any effort, and yet it is easily overlooked. You did not learn this 'being' from your parents or teachers at school, it was already there. And you did not have to make any effort to be. Being is available most naturally. And this space is for free. This aware being does not come and go, it has never been absent.

Q: Still I feel limited to my body and mind. This body is my house. There is a person inside here. Some call that the ego.

JK: Although we all seem to believe to be a person, the 'underlying' being has never been interrupted. And yet, most of us believe to be limited to a person because it *feels* that way. This sense of identification is so common that nobody seems to question it. But the ego is not something that was there from the beginning, it is added later. It is like a label they have put on your forehead. A label with your name on it. It is like a mask they have put on your face. It is not original to your being. It is a program on your computer which was added *after* you were born.

Q: Where did the sense of being a person come from then?

JK: Personhood is something you learned from your parents and teachers. And it took some time before this identification with the person became steady.

Q: As a newborn baby, there is no dualism yet?

JK: As a young baby, we don't make any separation yet between here and there, between inside the body and outside the body. There is absolutely no identification with the person yet. We are not influenced by the programs of our parents or by the customs of society. We have no sense of space or time. In the metaphor of the movie, we could say that there is just a white screen filled with images. There is no voice-over yet, there are no subtitles yet. In the metaphor of the cartoon, we could say that there is just a white paper filled with drawings, but no text balloons yet. Hunger, thirst, crying, eating, sleeping, they all just appear and disappear. We don't ask ourselves any questions yet. There is only presence. We simply *are*. At that very young age, we are pure openness without any labelling by inner voices. There are no comments yet on ourselves and no comments on the others around us. There is no division between me and the outside world. We are not programmed yet by education or religion.

Q: What does that mean?

JK: It means that there is a 'seeing' without interfering, a noticing without judging, a perceiving without expectations. There is no central character who claims to be the decider or the thinker or the doer. There is only a 'witnessing' without thinking in terms of me and the others, without any sense of past or future. We have no idea about here or there. We don't realize that we are a boy or girl with a specific nationality. We don't feel locked up in a body. We don't know about our gender. There are no borders. There are no voices in our head. There are no expectations. There is no ego on the stage who believes he or she needs to meet certain standards or follow certain rules. As a young baby, our computer hasn't been programmed yet – or the programs which are there are not activated yet. There is just pure being. Just is-ness. Just aware beingness.

Q: We are still unspoiled, unstained.

JK: But as we grow up, all sorts of programs are activated. It's like apps which are installed on our tablet or smartphone. Some are activated by our parents and teachers to feel comfortable in modern society. Our parents give us a name. But the baby couldn't care less. The young baby doesn't identify with that name or with its body. If you put a small white bandage or tape on the forehead of a baby and then put it in front of a mirror, it will not put his hand on the forehead to check the white spot on his face. There is no self-recognition yet. It will take some effort and perseverance from the parents to inject personhood into their child. When we are a bit older, they put us in front of a mirror and say that *we* are that person *they* see in the mirror. But we say, "He is my little friend behind the glass in the other bathroom." Yet, after a while we learn to identify ourselves with our name and our body. We accept to be a 'me' who is separate from the others. We accept to be limited to this person in this body because our parents keep saying that we are what *they* observe. They say that we are a person in a body. And although it takes a while, at some point we believe that, and we integrate that.

Q: All this is necessary to take part in society, isn't it?

JK: Yes, it is essential. But while we accept this new identity, we seem to 'lose' something more precious: we forget about the openness as a new-born. We seem to trade the original spaciousness for a limited sense of me. For example, we accept the border between 'me' and not-me.

Q: We lose our freedom and get locked up in the prison of a body and mind.

JK: Yes, but it only happens *apparently*. It's more like a hypnosis, we *think* we are in a body, but it is a thought we believe in. But the spaciousness never gets lost. During deep sleep, when the voices in the head are silent, the sense of spaciousness isn't covered up by these voices and habits. Then there is just spaciousness. But we don't remember that the next morning because our memory was also inactive.

Q: I see. But as soon as we wake up, the apps on our tablet are activated again. All the images appear again, memories come to life again, and we also see an image of our face when brushing our teeth in front of the mirror. And we give that image the subtitle, "I am this person, this is me." Maybe we also add a label to that face. Maybe we think, "I look a bit tired this morning." In other words, we have identified with a mask with certain characteristics.

JK: So, we have put on the mask of personhood. Underneath our mask, there is still the naked 'face' of our original aware beingness. It is still there, but remains unrecognized.

Q: The pure awareness is still there, but it is covered up by the mask we have received from our parents and teachers. And we believe that we *are* the mask.

JK: That is the collective hypnosis of humanity. We identify with our learned identity. We personalize the impersonal. Remember that as a young baby, we knew no boundaries. Life was spontaneous and impersonal, there was only open space. As adults, all sorts of boundaries are established in our mind.

Q: The division between me and the outside world is created, and it is taken for real.

JK. Yes. And all sorts of qualities are given to us. Sometimes we are described as a good boy or a good girl and rewarded for behaving in a certain way. Sometimes we seem to be bad according to our educators and then we are punished. This is one of the many ways to learn about the rules of the game of the adults. We must learn these rules because we need to be prepared to join modern society. We learn a language. We need to learn how to behave. We are told that we have a past and a future. We are told that we should make our lives work.

Q: As we grow up and identify more and more with our body and mind, we gradually accept to be a person in a body and we 'lose' our original openness as a new-born. But the open space is still here, uninterrupted.

JK: Right. We identify with the wave, but we forget that our true nature is the wetness of the ocean. But identification with the wave is not bad or so. The appearance of the ego is very practical in everyday life. But there is also a shadow side. We feel limited, as if there is something we have lost. Some people seem to miss this original openness at some point in their life. They feel that something is lacking. There might be a melancholy about a vague sense of freedom during early childhood. Because of this, some become philosophers or spiritual seekers.

Q: We know deep in our hearts that something crucial is missing. There is a gap, there's an emptiness inside. And we might feel an urge to fill that gap inside.

JK: Yes. And there are many ways to fill the gap. There are a few tracks which are presented in philosophy or religion to bring us back home. Different traditions have different pathways to bring us back to what we are or to fill that gap. There are a lot of tracks available, and there are also a lot of sidetracks. Some try to fill the gap by money or by affluence. Or by looking for power, success and respect in society. Others look for intellectual satisfaction through, for example, studying philosophy. Others find solace or distraction in music or art. Others give meaning to their lives by caring for their partner, children or parents. Some give deeper meaning to their lives by helping people in need in their direct environment or even in other areas of the world. But for some there is still a deep sense of lack after all. Maybe there is also a sense of insecurity, of melancholy, a sense of fear even. Some try to find a solution through therapy. Others try to find consolation or a deeper recognition in religion. Others try to find inner peace through mindfulness, yoga or meditation.

Q: Where does nondualism fit in here?

JK: Nondualism is not a tool to fill in the gap. It is not therapy. But it might bring clarity. As a result, we can differentiate between what we are and what we are not. It is not a way to find peace and happiness, although the sense of something lacking may disappear as a side effect of the clarity. When it's clear that what we really are is *the open space*, the sense of lack may dissolve. But it takes more than understanding nondualism intellectually.

Life seems to flow like a river,
and we all seem to be carried along
by the mighty power of the stream.
Some sages say to just let go,
to surrender to what is,
because the river of life
will take care of everything.
Most people, however,
swim against the flow.
They, too, are carried along
by the flow of life.
Nobody is excluded.

Person and Presence

Q: In your books, you distinguish between the human dimension and the universal dimension. Isn't that a new form of duality?

JK: Yes, of course it is. As human beings, we have a human aspect and a being aspect. This division between these two 'aspects' is obviously artificial and not really correct, but it is applied to make things clear. It is a compromise. The *human* aspect is our sense of being a person, the *being* aspect is our pure awareness. The first one is symbolized by the wave, the second one is symbolized by the ocean. The first one stands for our personal story, the second one refers to our timeless awareness. This aware beingness witnesses everything effortlessly but it is not separate from what it perceives. The metaphor of the ocean and the waves is interesting to illustrate that the wave is not on one side and the ocean on the other side. The wave is just a limited expression of the ocean, and is never separate from that ocean.

Q: The division between wave and ocean is also conceptual.

JK: Yes, indeed. A lot of books on philosophy, psychology and spirituality are mainly pointing to our human dimension. They are about you and me as separate persons, as individuals. They point to our individual stories, not to that common field which we all are. I try to point to the impersonal dimension, but without overlooking the human dimension. We can't deny the personal dimension. The feeling of being in a body can still appear, but it is only a feeling which lasts less than a second.

Q: I see.

JK: In some nondual traditions, the sense of being a person is described as illusory, or something to get rid of. I find it very natural to have a sense of personhood. One of the goals of some spiritual paths is to get into a state without ego. I don't think one needs to get rid of the ego, it will probably turn out to be the ego fighting the ego. One idea in our mind attacking another idea in our mind. If someone would claim to have destroyed the ego, it might just as well be one of his or her inner voices talking.

Q: It is meaningless. A wave comes into existence, but it isn't a problem for the ocean.

JK: I am not striving for an ocean without my wave.

Q: It seems difficult to destroy your ego.

JK: Like the snake which eats its own tail, it doesn't work. I believe it is enough to see that the ego is no more than an idea which pops up a few times a day. The ego is way overrated. The ego is more like a practical tool we need to function in society. I like the wave for what it is, I don't want to ignore it or fight it, I don't want to pretend it is not here, but the subject of my conversations is the ocean.

Q: Ok, I understand. But I have been going through a lot of misery and disappointments in my life over the last two years. Focusing on the ocean instead of on the waves is not going to be very helpful to me.

JK: Nondualism is not about you personally. And it is not about solving your problems. Nondualism points to the impersonal. It is only a matter of change in perspective. It is not about *improving* your life. I am not selling an upgrade of your person, I am just putting the wave in perspective. You pretend to be a wave and I remind you of your ocean-ness. That's all.

Q: And how can I apply this new perspective?

JK: When you have been going through storms of emotions or pain, and at some point, the storm is over, is there anything inside you which has *not* changed by that storm? Something which was there before the storm, during the storm and after the storm.

Q: My awareness.

JK: Yes, or even better, *the* awareness. I am referring to that which is beyond or before your identity, while at the same time it isn't separate from us. In nondualism, we point out the simplicity and the nakedness of the unchanging awareness which is not influenced by storms of strong emotions, by waves of pure joy or by huge tornadoes of physical pain. It is fully 'there' during both pain and joy.

Q: I haven't been able to recognize that awareness.

JK: You never will. It is the unfindable one. It is the unattainable one. And yet, this is what we all are.

Q: And I am that awareness.

JK: We are that awareness. Not you, *we*. Recognizing this is not an accomplishment.

Q: It is kind of strange, but I feel now a subtle sense of contentment coming from within. And being aware of this naked awareness seems to put in perspective my problems of the past as well. Maybe my problems were mainly thought based. Or at least made worse by my ideas about 'my' problems.

Nothing can get the person
out of its self-made prison,
because the idea of the person
is the prison.

The Seeker is Addicted to the Path

Q: What kind of path did you follow, and where did it bring you?

JK: I usually don't like to address such a question, because it focuses on the person instead of on the impersonal. Don't get distracted by looking at me *as a person*. Nondualism isn't really interested in the personal story. Still, my story may appear interesting for you *as a person*.

First, I must say that I haven't attained anything special at all. Maybe some teachers or masters have reached a very special state, but I haven't. I am not saying this because I am so humble or because I don't want to get a certain label. The character Jan simply hasn't reached anything special on the spiritual path. In other words, I am not dwelling in a higher state of awareness than you.

Q: Still, you wrote all these books.

JK: All you could say is that I seem to have lost some concepts I used to take seriously. Some old belief systems seem to have lost their power. I can't say why this happened or how it happened. It feels as if it happened *despite* of Jan, not because of Jan. It is true that I used to believe all the stories I read about the spiritual books from the East. I was in my twenties and I must admit that I was fascinated by these stories, and I thought at the time that I should reach such a state as well. And some things did happen in my story - if we accept for two minutes that past and future are real. There are many belief systems which have been unmasked along the way. But even this unmasking is something I can't claim.

Q: What are the concepts that you have unmasked then?

JK: The three major tools the spiritual seeker uses to survive are the belief in past and future, the belief in here and there, and the belief in high and low. These are the three major mechanisms of the ego to create dualism. I described these three tools in more detail in the book "This Is It". These three mechanisms are very practical to apply in daily life as a *human* being, and we should not discard them completely for that reason. But on the being 'level' these three tools become obsolete.

Q: How do you mean?

JK: On the human level, it is important to distinguish between past and future, between here and there, between my body here and your body over there, between driving through at a green traffic light or stopping your car for a red traffic light. But on the *being* level – which is not really a different level because the being level contains the human level – these three tools are not helpful at all. They confirm your sense of being a seeker on a path to the top of the mountain.

Q: I see. So, the nondualism you write about starts with a seeker but ends with the unmasking of that same seeker.

JK: The subject I talk about is not about me or you or a special state of a sage in India, but it refers to that aware beingness which doesn't exclude anyone. Much of my inspiration came from the East, like Buddhism, Taoism and Hinduism, but the ideas I want to share in my books are not related to any tradition at all.

Q: But you seem to have followed a certain path, haven't you?

JK: You see, the major problem with answering your question is that it suggests that the seeker – as a person – is on a path from a low level of consciousness to a high level of consciousness. And usually it is believed that certain techniques such as meditation facilitate this quest to attain this magical state which is described in several spiritual scriptures. I am not saying that there are no special states we can attain. I have travelled in many countries in Asia, I have met many teachers and masters and priests, I have been meditating for many years, and I have had several special experiences.

Q: So, it was helpful?

JK: In the apparent story, it may look as if these experiences were helpful. And one could say the same about the interesting teachers I met. The conversations brought a lot of clarity as well. So, I am not denying that.

Q: But most seekers still believe it is about their person who wants to reach a special state of peace and contentment *for themselves*.

JK: Realizing that eventually the seeker itself is not invited for the party, is not a pleasant discovery. When you identify yourself with a spiritual seeker, you feel you are on your way to the top of the mountain. And then you realize that you are not invited for this awakening party.

Q: At first, the seeker is disappointed?

JK: The spiritual seeker may be disappointed because he or she imagined having reached a certain level when compared to other beings who do not meditate or do not live according to a specific spiritual tradition. The spiritual ego may be proud about himself or herself. When it becomes clear that there is no hierarchy when it comes to beingness, it is difficult for the advanced spiritual seeker to accept that. The spiritual ego usually hates nondualism.

Q: That is why real nondualism is not very popular.

JK: The seeker may even become more disappointed when it becomes clear that the person we have learned to identify with, is never going to reach the ultimate. In other words, instead of looking for liberation for the person, it becomes clear that nondualism refers to liberation from the person. And this is completely unacceptable for the spiritual ego. Most seekers run away from this.

Why not simply rest
as awareness,
prior to any
conceptualisation?

Passionate About Nondualism

P: Why are you so passionate about nonduality and Advaita?

JK: I believe it is a subject that never fatigues the mind because the subject is *beyond* the mind. And the mind gets both fascinated and frustrated by that, because the mind knows that *something* is there – which some call an open secret – and on the other hand the mind feels very frustrated that it can't get its hands on it. You can never say, and I can't either, and nobody else can say, "I have got it. I have understood it. I've got it all. Now I have finished the job, I have all the understanding, I got my PhD in nonduality." You never get it.

P: It's not possible.

JK: You can write a book about it, and you can keep on talking about it, but you will always, in the end, have to admit, "I have failed." I failed in describing it, in understanding it, in feeling it. The only thing you can't fail is *being* it. And that is what we are all 'doing' anyway. That is the paradox. And this paradox will never leave you. And I think that is why you ask the question. This will never fatigue. This will never stop fascinating us. When you are a seeker, you feel something is lacking in life. In your ordinary day to day life, something is missing. Something that goes back to when you were three weeks old, that open awareness which was there. And when you grow up and reach the age of two or three, you get lost and you identify with the person you think you are, which *others* say you are.

At some point, you start to miss that open awareness. And then you become a seeker. And then, of course, you will go around and look for spirituality or philosophy to find answers to your questions. And some seem to give you answers, others don't. And you keep on searching. Those who really want to know and don't want to make any compromises, might end up in Advaita. And even there, the frustration will go on because this is a subject which – as I said before - cannot be reached by a person. In a way, you could say that the person is standing in the way. On the other hand, the person is not standing in the way because it is there anyway. It's full of paradoxes: one moment I will say this and five minutes later I will say the opposite and both will be true.

P: Yes

JK: This is something readers of Advaita will have to get used to. When you read a book about conventional philosophy you just know that there is a very intelligent person writing down a story and that all of it goes as it should go. But in Advaita you will have these contradictions all the time.

P: There are quite a few people nowadays who speak about Advaita, and sometimes they also point at each other, and say, "He's got it wrong, I got it right." Can you get this wrong?

JK: No, of course not. I agree with you. In one of my books I have done something similar, by saying that someone was not a real Advaita teacher because he was compromising. And I suggested that in some interviews. But afterwards I should always say, "In the end, it doesn't matter." In the end, nobody is wrong or right about this. Nonduality means that there is no division between left and right, high and low, me and you. Where would I find the inspiration to say that this person is 'less' than the other one? So even when someone is obviously compromising, then that is what's happening. That's the expression of beingness – or the nondual reality or energy of life, whatever you want to call it.

To deny that one exists
is unnatural and foolish.
To know that one *is*,
is natural and obvious.
This knowing takes
no effort or special skills.

Black and White

Q: One of the things that bothers me about nonduality is that some teachers say that there is no good without bad.

JK: The Taoists already knew how important it is to see that the bright and the dark exist within each other. These two are in a constant flux, like white and black on their famous taijitu. This symbol refers to the Chinese concept of yin and yang, of opposites existing in complete harmony. It is also remarkable that these opposites are also the source for each other, visualized by a white dot within the black part and a black dot within the white area.

Q: Still, I can't accept that life is a dream and that judging is not allowed. What kind of society would that lead to? It seems all very real to me. And judging is important is society.

JK: First we need to remember that those people who write about nondualism are sometimes misunderstood. What they say is mainly applicable to the absolute level. The nondual space knows no good or bad. And for a spiritual seeker who gets into touch with nondualism, the sense of balance between good and bad is mainly applied on the spiritual level. For example, in nondualism, the concept of heaven and hell loses its significance completely.

Q: Ok, the spiritual ego doesn't believe any more in good and bad when it comes to religion and spirituality. I can accept that, although I know a lot of religious people will never accept your theory at all. They will probably say that your philosophy of oneness is dangerous. But I am fine with that. However, what about not judging in everyday life in normal society? What do these sages have to say about that?

JK: When they are referring to everyday life, these wise men and women will surely put their words in perspective. They will not ask you to kill people because nondualism says that there is no good or bad. However, the clarity on the spiritual level may have certain consequences or side effects on the social level as well. Now I am talking about this subject as if time and evolution are real, but I have no other option when explaining it. They will say that nondualism leads to less labelling of people. The thinking mind becomes quieter, the voices inside our heads which always judge and criticize, become less important. So, one becomes less rigid in the mind.

Q: I can see that nondualism leads to less labelling. And if I understand this balance between black and white, I am fighting less against the black side of life. And when one has undermined the idea of good and bad on the spiritual level, one also starts to apply that insight on the everyday level. It is like a sort of nice side effect of the clarity, right? One becomes gradually less judgmental on the social level as well. Is that correct? The seeker has unmasked the little voices inside her or his head, and that brings peace of mind on all levels.

JK: The voices inside our heads have less impact, less authority. The nondual wisdom may also lead to the idea that everything is always in a flux, and that there can't be black without white. However, knowing that north and south are always in balance doesn't imply that you don't have to stop your car for a red light any more. The rules of society still apply. But when these books of nondualism say that there is no good without bad, they mainly point to the spiritual field, and they also point to the fact that the good and the bad are mainly in our heads.

Q: And when one is absorbed in presence, when all the voices in the head are quiet or almost quiet, any question about changing the future or changing other people seems obsolete. Even the imperfections of the world are part of the whole. Everything is as it is, because it is as it is.

JK: And this may sound indifferent to some people who are not familiar with this, but it might also be the opposite. Some describe the impersonal neutral witness as the 'beloved' or as unconditional love. This is a natural outcome, especially when you see that your awareness and the awareness of your enemy are the same space.

A path is designed
to cross the distance
between two different areas.
But which path is available
to go from ego to presence?
From wave to ocean?

Postnondualism

Q: What do you mean by Postnondualism?

JK: Postnondualism is not some new philosophy. And it isn't a new tradition in the field of nonduality. It simply describes what some seekers have experienced 'after' having the full 'understanding' of nondualism.

Q: These seekers are already familiar with the nondual texts of, for example, Zen, Advaita, Ch'an or Dzogchen, to name a few.

JK: One can also find nondual wisdom in ancient Western traditions, of course. Or in the Middle East. But I am not interested in how this nondualism is expressed in each tradition. That is only a side track for the seeking mind. I am only interested in the common field.

Q: You point to that which is *universal* knowledge. You try to describe this nondual wisdom in its naked form. A vision which is stripped from all the local interpretations, terms and symbols.

JK: So, when these people are clear about that which all these nondual texts agree upon, we might say that they are familiar with the true core of nondualism. Naked nondualism. It can be formulated without using any terms from the East. Nondualism is not about oneness, it points to 'not two-ness.' It is very simple to understand. So, these people have found out that there is no past and future, no here and there, no high and low, no me and them, because all these are concepts in our minds. They have looked for the person inside 'their' head, heart or belly, and couldn't find any personality. There is indeed nobody home. Even during surgery, we never found a little person in the brain.

The seeker is checkmated. There is nowhere to go. We can't premeditate our own disappearance, we can't plan our own liberation. If the seeker can't be identified, how could we bring him or her into a higher state? If time is a concept, how could liberation be projected into a future state? We can't premeditate our own disappearance, we can't plan our own liberation. Everything else we say is a compromise. According to nondualism, everything is just *happening*.

Q: Now I understand that naked nondualism is never going to be very popular. It is way too frustrating for a seeker to find out that you are cornered.

JK: Or even worse, you just found out that you are not invited for the party in heaven. Maybe you thought you didn't enter yet because you were not good enough, because you were not wearing the right robes. Because you were still hiding a few sins under your garment. But here in naked nondualism one may find out that you will not enter because that 'you' doesn't exist.

Q: I see. I believe some seekers would start to scratch their head now.

JK: What we really are, deep down, is the unlimited space which is the core and fabric of existence itself. And at the same time, it is also true that nothing is really happening. Nondualism makes it clear that the 'what is' is both everything and nothing. That is the true meaning of naked nondualism. No more separation between this and that. I can say this to you in this conversation because I know you are familiar with nondualism. However, saying to people that everything is nothing will raise many eyebrows, especially when you are talking to, for example, a professor in psychology. And these statements – which are very common in naked nondualism – expose the futile plan of the spiritual ego to find personal liberation in the future. This might come as a major disappointment, especially to the serious spiritual seeker who has invested a lot of time and belief in his religious or spiritual career.

Q: When does postnondualism come in then?

JK: In postnondualism, all the insights of naked nondualism are still recognized as true on the absolute level, but the sense of being a person is not neglected or suppressed, it is rather celebrated for what it is. It is not overrated any more, nor underrated. The wave is seen for what it is. One can feel like being a separate person for a short moment and at the same time the impersonal aware beingness is recognized as 'unbroken.' And it is not recognized by you but by itself. For some seekers, this insight brings an end to their battle against personhood. Others might believe it is only a light version of real nondualism. And the latter is true from a theoretical point of view. But such opinions are not so important, they also come and go in the same nothingness which is everything.

Q: I used to have the crazy idea that I should - permanently - be in a superconscious state of egoless bliss. I secretly hoped to become like one of the great masters from India, China or Japan. And as I failed to do be like them most of the time, despite my meditations and my efforts to live a strict spiritual life, I regarded this as a failure. And that sense of failure was the origin of even more frustrations. And this seemed to create even more ego. So, I was in a constant battle against the so-called evil forces of my ego. It felt as if I was beating my own head with a hammer. I couldn't stay in the egoless state for very long. It was so frustrating. Then it was such a relief to read your article on postadvaita. I realized that all this wasn't necessary. Let's say that I have freed myself from chasing a spiritual fantasy.

JK: There is no need to fight your ego. And who would be doing that? The sense of being a person is just an old habit popping up. It has no importance. It is only an idea which appears for a very short time, usually less than a second, several times a day. Most of the time, there is just is-ness *without* the image of being a person. The ego is way overrated. This image is not what you are. Mind the difference between what we really are and what we think we are.

Q: I see. I shouldn't pay attention to this ego any more. If I got this right, postnondualism means that the seeker has achieved the complete clarity that the personality is illusory, but also sees that the sense of personhood is allowed again. You don't need to try and attain a special state without an ego. When this is seen through, that battle is over.

JK: There is no need to deny the ego to recognize that the impersonal spaciousness arises in everything. No need to stop the mind. No need to fight the senses. No need to change our diet. No need to stop enjoying sensuality or sexuality. No need to get rid of material wealth. No need to shave your head and become celibate. But if you are a monk or a nun, that is also an expression of oneness. No need to criticize that. There are no rules. And no requirements. No need to copy the spiritual heroes. No need to change your garment. No need to sleep on a bed with iron nails. No need to wait for the enlightenment bus. No need to wait until the sense of ego drops away. One doesn't have to suppress the wave to recognize the ocean. So, it is not either/or but both/and. It is a complementary view. No need to forget the wave in order to become wet, both ocean and wave are expressions of oneness.

Q: In other words, postnondualism says that having a sense of being a person in a body is not wrong, it is only a sense which pops up in our mind a few times a day. It's no more than that. We are an ocean which thinks a few times a day to be one wave. And that is fine.

JK: It's only our memory which makes the ego look solid and continuous. It's like the sound of a bell, it's gone within a few moments. And that bell is not ringing continuously. Don't believe me, check it out. It's like the bells of a church which ring every hour during a few seconds, they are not ringing twenty-four hours a day. So, most of the day, these bells are silent. Clearly seeing that, is enough. This clarity brings the ego or the personality to its real proportions. No need to deny it, no need to overrate it, there is just seeing it for what it is. A concept which pops up a few times a day. At that point, it is even obsolete to say that there is nobody home. Who would be saying that the sense of ego dropped away? Everything just is. Everything is just happening. Isn't that amazing? How simple.

Q: In other words, postnondualism is not asking the seeker to attain an ultra-conscious state of 'always being nobody'. So, I can allow my dark sides as well. I don't have to follow an ideal. I don't have to be in a continuous peaceful state of mind. Oh God, I am so relieved that I can release the hounds now.

JK: You don't have to play a role any more. No need to act spiritual or holy. But be vigilant. Don't turn this new insight into a new strategy. There is no need to detox from your bad habits or to get rid of your old emotional injuries. Lots of healers will be more than happy to help you with that. It is not forbidden to get healing, it may be interesting on the human level. But it is pointless on the being level. It is not needed to become who you are. There are no conditions. It is just this.

Q: The voices in my head were already soliciting for new business, like getting rid of all my old injuries and personal issues. But that's not necessary. Healing is not needed because that would be *personal* healing again. And I don't have to pretend to be special on the spiritual realm either. That's a huge relief for me.

JK: One doesn't have to reside in a special state continuously, because that would be a goal for the spiritual ego. If you believe that you can attain this ideal state, you confirm the existence of the person. Again, it would give the ego to much credit. It would give the wave to much importance. No effort is needed. You as a wave will never be able to 'do' it, and you as the ocean are already being it. It has nothing to do with the person at all. Pointing to the wave will not bring more clarity to this issue, only pointing to the ocean could do that. And I should add here that my words are not capable of pointing to the ocean.

Q: You once said in an interview that you can't point to oneness, and yet wherever you point at is fine.

JK: Yes, nothing can be pointed at as *the* source of everything, but the 'spaciousness' in which the pointing happens is what my conversations are trying to point to. But don't believe that I have *attained* that. It is not about Jan, it is not about me. It is about all of us, and beyond that. It is beyond anything the mind can imagine. Zen Buddhists say, "Don't examine the finger pointing at the moon." Don't look at the piano player, only listen to the music and check out what the music is referring to. I will sometimes point to 'your' true nature, I will point to 'your' moon light, while it isn't yours at all. But don't examine my finger, don't even examine the moon. I am only trying to point to the sun which is the source of the moon light. The moon has no light of its own, although the moon might pretend it does. The real source is the sun. That sounds a bit like I point now to a source which is one step earlier, or one step subtler. But there is no 'one step earlier' of course. And even the metaphor of the sun is misleading. This light has no central origin because it is everywhere. The sun in this metaphor can't be seen. That is why I like the term 'aware spaciousness' because a space sounds neutral and impersonal. And this space has no center.

Some seekers report
that they experienced
states of bliss and peace,
and seem to be convinced
that such events should
be continued every day.
But can the intermittent ever
experience the timeless?
What if our most ordinary
sense of being is already 'it'?

Everything is Just Happening

Q: Many teachers say that everything is just happening of its own accord. Like an autopilot. They also say that life is a movie which is as insubstantial as a dream at night.

JK: Yes, but with the daytime 'dream,' there is no seeker who is waking up *out of* the dream. What we are referring to in nondualism is the recognition of our true nature without going from one place to another. No need to evolve from one stage to a next stage. Recognizing the aware space is waking *into* the dream. There was a Woody Allen film in the eighties, The Purple Rose of Cairo, where a character stepped out of the movie. We all know that this is not possible. Nobody can step out of the story of his or her life. It is the same for the spiritual seeker, you can't say that you stepped out of your life. That is simply another image on the white screen.

Q: But isn't that what most spiritual seekers are trying to do? To leave behind the limitation of personhood to step into another world of peace and silence?

JK: Yes, but there isn't anything outside the movie. The movie in our metaphor isn't watched from outside like in a real movie where the viewer is watching a white screen with images. We are looking 'from inside', because the movie is three dimensional. And we are not separate from the space we are in. And this space has no limits, so this 'box' has no emergency exit in the back. And I need to add here that we are not really inside the box *as an entity*, because that entity itself is also part of our belief in space and personhood.

Q: Can I get a sense of that infinite box of awareness by meditating or practicing yoga? Why are most seekers meditating, and what is it good for? You once said that it is not necessary to meditate twice a day, but you also don't invite people to stop their meditation. I know that many Buddhist traditions use meditation as a tool, along with other spiritual techniques. Some say that during meditation they discovered the inner source of true contentment. Instead of looking for happiness in the outside world or in the realm of sense perceptions or in the field of the conceptual world, they have found a fountain of happiness *inside*. They claim that they have found a deeper happiness which is not generated by thoughts, feelings or experiences. A sense of inner contentment which can't be achieved by power or money. A sense of unconditional love which even relationships can't provide. They also say that in deep meditation, when there is pure silence, there is awareness of awareness. All that sounds very attractive to me. It reminds me also of what you describe in your books. What is the view of postnondualism on this subject?

JK: One can start with wondering why we are meditating. It is different for each one of us, and our motivation may even change over time. We can meditate because we have heard it is healthy for our body. For example, meditation can regulate our autonomic nervous system. For some people, it could regulate blood pressure or calm down the gastrointestinal tract. Some medical studies have found that meditation has a lot of benefits on both the physical and mental level. Researchers have found many benefits of both mindfulness meditation as well as transcendental meditation. They can be interesting in the field of cardiovascular diseases, depression, chronic pain, and so on. We can also meditate because we have heard it is good for stress related complaints.

Q: I believe it is better to meditate than to take medication for depression, high blood pressure, anxiety or a gastric ulcer.

JK: Yes, of course. But sometimes medical treatment is necessary. We can't generalize. But meditation goes far beyond the medical realm, and that is where it gets even more interesting. We can learn meditation to make us conscious about all the voices in our heads which are barking like wild dogs. For some people, that is a huge discovery. Mindfulness meditation courses are very interesting for that. It has become quite popular over the last decades. I recommend it sometimes to my patients, especially when they are too often 'living in their heads.'

Q: But there is more, right? In Zen and Transcendental Meditation, meditation is designed to go *beyond* the mind.

JK: Most people don't know what we are talking about here, when you say that you go *beyond* the mind. One of the reasons might be that they have no conscious awareness of naked consciousness which is beyond or before the mind and the five senses. I guess that, for example, Zen meditation, TM, yoga and tai chi can have interesting effects in that sense.

Q: I see. This sounds interesting.

JK: Don't draw any conclusions, please. It is true that a lot of people who are reading my books on nondualism, have a background of meditation, tai chi or yoga. But that doesn't mean that meditation leads to nondualism. Let's not put the cart in front of the horses. I prefer to describe the clarity as a *side effect* of meditation.

Q: Oh.

JK: But the danger is that now the spiritual ego will use the meditation as a technique to get to the clarity it wants so much.

Q: Then they are back on the spiritual path. And the ego is behind the steering wheel again.

JK: The ego is always hungry. It always needs new food to survive. So, it will always look for a new way to stay alive. Becoming a good yogi or an experienced meditator are one of the options.

Q: So, should I stop meditating then?

JK: No, because that would be a new decision, coming from the seeking ego. You stop mediating because you read in a book of nondualism that mediation is not necessary or even contra productive. If that is your motivation, you are still on the path. Just continue with meditating. Maybe you will get exhausted or so frustrated that it stops by itself. Maybe it continues. It doesn't matter.

Q: It is frustrating.

JK: Check out to whom it is frustrating. And realize that a sense of frustration doesn't change the space.

Q: All right. I got it.

JK: But again, many seekers confirm that mediation can bring them peace of mind, and make them aware of a transcendent field which is not recognized by most other people. That is also fine.

Q: But we should not use meditation as a tool to get somewhere.

JK: If pure consciousness has been 'seen' (by itself) one single time, the games of the spiritual ego can be unmasked. And theoretically, 'after' that insight, mediation is no longer necessary. But if there is still some doubt, you can meditate again to confirm the silence and spaciousness of pure awareness. The white lines between the human level and the being level become transparent.

Q: I see. In that way, 'we' get a view of the light of pure awareness.

JK: 'We' can also discover that there is no meditator who is doing the mediation. It may become clear that there is no yogi who is performing the yoga. Instead of 'practicing' yoga, we are 'being' it. We are yoga. Instead of 'practicing' meditation, we *are* meditation. Instead of experiencing naked awareness, we are 'being' naked awareness. Instead of being aware *of something*, there is just awareness. Just simple everyday awareness.

Q: It sounds too simple to be true.

JK: I believe if it would be complicated, it would be a trick from the thinking mind. Simplicity can be great. I believe Leonardo da Vinci said, "Simplicity is the ultimate sophistication." But simple doesn't mean it is easy for the seeking mind.

Q: The spiritual ego always looks for a new escape route. But meditation can also unmask the belief in the ego, isn't it?

JK: During the meditation, when the parrots in our head are having a siesta, we recognize the 'naked' awareness which was there all the time. And this 'normal' awareness seems to continue after the meditation. The white paper on which our comic of life is drawn becomes apparent, and after the meditation the white paper is still there. And the drawing of our ego was only a few black lines on that same white paper. So, it becomes clear that the person inside our body was only a concept. For some seekers, this insight might have interesting consequences. It might bring an end to their spiritual longing. We are not on the level of techniques any more, we are not aiming for a specific goal any more. Why is that? Because there is no doer of the technique. It becomes very simple.

We may still meditate or do yoga *after* that insight because it feels good, because it is healthy, because it brings a peaceful moment in this busy world, or because it reminds us of what we really are. But once it is clear that the sense of separateness is just an idea which pops up a few times a day, it is no longer used as a tool to reach a spiritual goal.

Q: Why is that?

JK: Because the one who needs to get there has been unmasked. And so, it becomes clear that the car is driving without a driver behind the steering wheel. But I will never ask you to stop yoga or meditation, because that would be another task. I would be talking to the seeker again. If I would say that meditation is counterproductive, that would also address the seeking ego. I would give too much attention to that personality. But if meditation or yoga still happens, it happens. It's perfectly fine. It doesn't matter. And if it doesn't happen anymore, it doesn't happen anymore. And if ten years later you pick it up again, then that is what is happening. But the idea that meditation will bring the ego to the final goal is seen through.

Q: However, the identification with the body and mind remains to some extent.

JK: Yes, and we need some identification to be able to function in society. If your partner calls your name, and asks you if you want some more tea, you are turning your head to your friend and you automatically respond with yes or no, aren't you? If a seeker calls a teacher of nonduality a question during a retreat, he is immediately turning his head to that person, isn't he? Even when that same teacher just said five minutes earlier that there is nobody here while pointing to himself or herself, this basic sense of personhood remains.

Q: It is the core of the human part of the human being.

JK: This basic identification is a program that should not be removed from your computer. It is part of the operating system of your laptop, don't erase it. But it is only a program. The ego is a file which pops up several times a day, and because of memory it seems as if it is continuously in the middle of the action. And it really feels as if the ego is behind the steering wheel. We just *pretend* we are persons. Everybody else is also pretending, whether they realize that or not. What can be wrong if that sense would reappear a few times a day? It is like the bells of a church which ring every hour. But as said before, there is no need to fight against that ego, that would give it to much importance.

Q: And there is also no need to tell others that you live without an ego. No need to impose your 'discovery' to others.

JK: It's another trick of the mind. That statement would be another voice of the ego mind. Whether you are talking to others or to yourself, it is obsolete. No need to say to yourself there is no you.

Q: Claiming that one has no more ego would rather be a sophisticated form of denial, isn't it?

JK: It's not necessary to say such a thing. Who would be saying that? Yet, something has been seen through. It is not a form of madness. It is not a mental disease. It is rather the opposite, we don't believe the voices in our heads anymore which say that we are limited to this personal identity. The ego is simply seen for what it is. That's all.

Q: As you said earlier, it is just an idea which pops up a few times a day.

JK: Yes. And memory pretends that the ego is there 24 hours a day, while it isn't. In other words, it is no longer given more value than it really deserves. The most spread conditioning is that we are a person who is conscious and who is living in a body. We also believe that consciousness is limited to the body, that it resides in the brain and that it limits itself to the shape and size of the body. Because of this limitation, our mind set also becomes limited and egotistical, focusing on our life as this person. And it feels as if we are the center of our story. We believe we are the thinker of our thoughts, the feeler of our emotions, the doer of our deeds. And that is how we are programmed. We may also be in a hurry, because we know that this life is limited in time, because we stay on this planet for an average of about 80 years or so. This sense of identification with personhood is fine when it comes to taking care of our body like eating, drinking and sleeping. And we need it for our social interactions in society. But this is a limited aspect of consciousness, it is only the personal version of consciousness. This human version of consciousness is part of a 'bigger' consciousness which has no limits.

Q: And I *am* that. I am that universal consciousness.

JK: What you just said is correct, but it felt like you were talking from memory. It didn't sound fresh. The words of others can inspire you, of course. To confirm it mentally is one thing, to really see and feel it is the essence of nondual wisdom. Well, you can't really see that universal awareness like you see an object, that is the paradox. Words fail to describe this. The person can't *do* this seeing or feeling. The awareness we all identify with on an individual level is not separate from that big awareness. It is a part of it, like waves are part of the ocean.

Q: So, there is a small consciousness in my brain and a big consciousness outside?

JK: I wouldn't put it that way. One is not separate from the other. The big one is also 'inside' you, and it also 'around' you. It is one substance. It is one awareness. And it is not aware *of* something, it is just aware. The 'small' awareness in my brain and the 'big' awareness outside are made of the same basic ingredients. It sounds weird when we first hear this, but your awareness and my awareness are not apart, they are one and the same. There is no separation.

The mind of the 'spiritual seeker'
will always try to postpone
the recognition of what-is.
How?
By suggesting that
there is a path to follow.
Why?
Because it believes
that the actual what-is
isn't the 'real' what-is (yet).

The Absence of Separation

Q: The absence of separation is a major thing in nondualism. All there is, is one aware ocean.

JK: Where is the demarcation line between wave and ocean? Isn't that white line in our minds as well? It is like road markings. For some people the separation between me and you is a double white line. And the line between past and future is only a single line. Maybe during meditation this white line becomes a dotted line, and sometimes the line disappears all together. We may also realize that all these white lines – double or single, dotted or not dotted – were only in our minds. Anyway, a double white line between your awareness and my awareness can't be found. On the deeper level, we are already one and the same ocean.

Q: I guess this is only true for the deeper level of the ocean. On the surface there is still separation, isn't it?

JK: There is no dualism between the surface of the ocean and its deeper layers. Where is the border line between the waves on the surface and the so-called deeper layers of the ocean? It is all made of water molecules. I used that image to explain things, but that duality is a conceptual demarcation line in our heads as well. So, no white line between up and down either.

Q: How can we see this?

JK: You can't see it, that plan will never work out. You - as a person - will never see it, but you - as pure awareness - *are* already it. So, the person can't do anything. But the ego always wants to go to the next level. The spiritual ego wants to do something to get there. That is not going to happen. See if we can sit here for two minutes without aspirations, without requests. Accept that no effort is needed for two minutes. It's not as easy as it sounds, your ego will turn even this experiment into a new task. It will call it the 'no-effort' exercise. Why not stay here and simply be? Leave everything else, ignore all paths which take a step. Don't listen to the voices in your head. No need to make any effort at all.

Q: I just allow that which takes no effort at all. I let everything be as it is, there's nothing to change or to heal. And if change or healing happens, that is also an expression of oneness.

JK: No need for effort, no next step is necessary. We just stay as we are. And I know these words sound as if I am inviting you to be in a certain way. It looks to the seeker that I am giving you something to do, while I said before that this ego doesn't exist as a solid entity. But let's just pretend for two minutes that there is a person who would be able to answer my questions and be without expectations. Remain as what remains, in and as that space which cannot be left aside. And when I say 'remain' as awareness, that is even obsolete because there is no way you can 'not remain' as awareness. And the 'me' who should be doing this, can't be found, so I should keep my mouth shut.

Q: It is a paradox.

JK: Awareness doesn't want to be anything else. Nobody is staying here. Just to 'stay here' without any attributes, is sometimes described as our natural state. But in the end, no description will cover this. Even making effort is included. No exercise or experiment can bring us closer to what we already are. No need to think or talk about naked awareness. No need to protect this space. Can this awareness fade away?

Q: No.

JK: You in your nakedness are already awake but your mask (which you think you are) is only a self-image. Still you put a lot of effort in that mask. You invest a lot of energy in your image. Most people worry a lot about how others look at them. They are living a life of an actor in the spotlights. They are conscious about how other people are looking at their mask. As if they are filmed by drones from all sides. It takes a lot of energy to keep up appearances.

But this image is not what we really are. It's only a thin mask.

Q: Where did the mask come from?

JK: It is only a concept, it is not solid and real in the traditional sense. Our parents gave this mask the name of our ego, like Jan or Chris. And we have taken over that concept. And we take it for real, and that belief seems to stay for decades. The ego is just a creation in the brain which imagines a sense of private consciousness. The ego claims things to be 'me' and imagines it to be separate from the rest, from the other 'egos.' It imagines a private bubble in which the rest of the world can be noticed. It claims its existence as its own personal private existence. But is-ness is just this, and that is whatever presents itself, and it doesn't need a concept called me to be what it is.

Q: And seekers are trying to find liberation *for* their mask?

JK: Yes. This mask cannot reach awareness, while the naked 'you' underneath the mask *is* already 'it.' It's as simple as that. And we go around in circles to find our self. That is the situation a lot of seekers find themselves in. They project themselves in the periphery, running after a self-created goal. While the centre of the wheel remains still, untouched and unseen.

Q: And this ego creates all sorts of way out.

JK: But the ego is not essential for anything. There is no me needed to take in these words, there is no me needed to say these words. There is no me needed to turn the pages when reading a book, there is no me needed to make a cup of tea, it is just an idea which is connected to our decisions and deeds afterwards.

Q: In many Advaita books they also say that there is no me. How can I know that this is true?

JK: But it can't be known that there is no me, that is another paradox in nondualism. We can know that there is a *sense* of me, but a *sense* of me is not a proof of the *existence* of a solid me. It is just a sense, a kind of feeling. And as I said before, that sense is only an image passing by for a very short moment. An image which passes by on a regular basis doesn't have any continuous quality. It is not permanent.

Q: Yet, in postnondualism, we know it is impermanent, but we allow ourselves to *pretend* to be a person.

JK: We all pretend to be a me continuously, even when we are sure that 'our' me is not permanent and that it can't be found. We can pretend that others also 'have' a permanent me inside their body mind - even when we are sure that their me is only a concept with no permanence at all.

Everyone says 'I' all the time,
like I am, I hope, I do, I want.
But what does this 'I' really mean?
Could this I be the one without a second?

Just Everyday Consciousness

Q: What is so fascinating about beingness?

JK: Just to be is a mystery, just beingness. Beingness is a magical word because nobody is excluded, everybody is 'doing' it. And it is being done naturally, we don't have to put any effort into this. It is completely natural to just sit on a chair and have no reflections while taking in these words. Did you notice how simple this is? There is just listening, sitting, breathing. There is no me needed for all this.

Q: There is no me needed for listening, sitting, breathing. Is it all impersonal then?

JK: During my last two sentences, while you were simply taking in my words as a neutral receptor, were you able to sit there without reflections about yourself, without any expectations regarding your spiritual quest?

Q: Yes, I was.

JK: And have you noticed if there was awareness of the qualities and characteristics of your so-called ego?

Q: No. I wasn't aware of the characteristics of my ego while I was simply listening. I was just sitting on a chair and taking in your words effortlessly. I wasn't even aware of something special, I was just aware. Simple everyday awareness.

JK: And everybody is 'doing' this naturally, you don't need to sit in lotus position to do this. No need to shave your hair or wear an orange robe to be able to do this.

Q: You don't have to be 'spiritual' or so. And you don't have to behave religiously. It is just ordinary aware beingness.

JK: Maybe you have pain, maybe you have frustrations, maybe you feel fine, maybe you feel balanced or in peace, it doesn't matter to beingness. And you don't expect anything to happen in the next two minutes. Just this. Your normal everyday consciousness is already 'it'. It has never been away. Where would it go if it is all-inclusive? Where would *you* go to find it? What would you do to improve it?

Q: There is nowhere to go.

JK: Once that is clear, a lot of those old programs and expectations disappear. Like, I should be more peaceful inside, I should be more like that spiritual hero. I am not good enough for this. The parrots in your head who used to repeat these words, are unmasked.

Q: Yesterday I had had an argument with my partner, and so I concluded afterwards, "I am not there yet, I should always be in peace." Now I realize that such a conclusion is ridiculous.

JK: No need to feed these types of thoughts. And no need to fight them, it's endless.

Q: Just to be. That's all.

JK: And this beingness is simple. But it is not simple in the sense that nothing is happening. You don't become a boring person, you don't become lazy.

Q: You don't stay in your bed whole day.

JK: You don't turn your back to society or to your fellow people. It has nothing to do with you as a person. Life goes on, spontaneously. It can be quite an adventure. Isn't it amazing that life is happening? Thousands of thoughts and emotions and sense perceptions pass by every day. Life is happening anyway, whether you like it or not, whether you want to control it or not. The movie is running, images are passing by, subtitles may appear, and still there is no director. The laws of nature seem to produce winter and summer, night and day, hot and cold. Planets are moving around the sun, subatomic particles are moving or vibrating. It is an essential characteristic of life. Life is simply flowing, everything is in a flux. The Greek Philosopher

Heraclitus said, "Pantha Rei", everything is always moving, like water in a river. Nothing stays the same. The Buddhists refer to it as the impermanence of things. Heraclitus also said that opposite things are identical. High and low, night and day, female or male, both are two sides of the same coin. There is always a subtle balance, although the balance may not be obvious when having a narrow point of view.

Q: Taoists refer to that as the balance between Yin and Yang. There is even a black dot in the white area and a white dot in the black area, meaning that the origin of white is in the black and the origin of black is in the white. That understanding brought me peace of mind. There is always a balance, and it is always taking new shapes because that circle of the Yin Yang symbol is always turning around.

JK: Yes. And when you see that, life just flows. Without any specific effort. And yet, things get done. You don't stay in your bed all day.

Q: Taoists call this Wu Wei, you do without feeling to be the doer. No need for a me to be able to breath, eat, talk or work. The laws of nature will take care of that.

JK: There is a natural ease that comes from this, we are milder towards others and ourselves. We seem to go along with the good moments and the bad moments more fluently because the tendency to label the pleasant thoughts as good and the unpleasant thoughts as bad lessens naturally. Your human expression will still prefer the pleasant moments because that is how the body and mind are programed, but the tendency to label black as bad and white as good is usually less. You realize now that these are only labels in your mind. The old tendency to project yourself in the past or in the future may still happen, but it will be a story within the story. And the spiritual search seems to lose its power.

The most frustrating journey
for the spiritual ego is trying
to get rid of the ego.

Teacher and Seeker

Q: One of the things that bothers me massively is that certain Indian masters are so popular that people start to worship them as if they are divine beings. I run away from that because I don't feel comfortable while seeing that on YouTube. On the other hand, I talked with people who were on a retreat with such a master, and they had gained a lot of insights in his presence. They also experienced authentic moments of deep recognition and clarity. So, I am a bit hesitant about how I should cope with this. I feel I have a deep desire to devote myself to something or someone. I am attracted to go and see such gurus, but I also have some pride inside me. What would my husband and colleagues say if they would see me bowing for an Indian master? What is going on in these places?

JK: You see, this is a nice example to illustrate the difference between duality and dualism. Duality is the difference between the person in the front who is the teacher, say of mathematics, and his or her audience, the pupils listening to him or her to learn the basics of mathematics. From an outsider's point of view, the teacher is standing in front of the classroom and the pupils are sitting in the rest of the room. That separation is duality. And it is totally fine.

In spiritual circles, a similar situation may occur. There is a duality between the master on the one hand and the followers on the other hand. That is again totally fine, it is just a distinction made by the mind. And if there are a lot of followers, it is normal that the teacher is sitting on a platform so that everybody can see him or her. When a spiritual leader like the Dalai Lama gives a speech to the United Nations, it is also similar. And people can be touched by his words on many levels as well.

Q: So where does the dualism come in then?

JK: Dualism may originate in the mind of the follower when he or she labels the teacher as higher than himself or herself. It may be a matter of gratefulness, respect and loyalty towards the teacher. And if you have had special experiences during a meeting with that teacher, your devotion and respect may become even more important. All this is fine. But in some circles, the master is described as an enlightened being, or a divine being, which could give the impression that the master is on a higher level than his devotees.

Q: This becomes even more obvious when people are bowing for the master or kneeling to kiss his or her feet.

JK: In spiritual circles, masters or gurus are likely to be labeled with divine qualities. I am not saying that they don't have special gifts. People say that when the master enters the room, the energy is uplifted.

Some of them are really unique beings. I am not judging this behavior. I am not saying that worshipping the master is bad or ridiculous. It is also an expression of oneness. But I understand that this devotion disturbs you. If you go to India, you see it in many places. There it is more common. I have been around several masters myself, and I learned a lot about devotion and the effects of being in a group of people who have a similar interest. It can be very powerful.

Q: Devotion or Bhakti is also one of the three ways in yoga to find liberation. To me, these masters are on a higher level of consciousness than their followers.

JK: According to nondualism, this is *not* the case. The master may obviously have certain qualities and talents which makes him or her to a master. This may be charisma, clarity, eloquence, intelligence, compassion, leadership, and much more. In nondualism, we still notice the difference. Especially when you listen to the conversations between master and follower, it may become obvious that the master really masters the subject while the devotee still lacks understanding and clarity. That difference is usually clear. It is a bit more difficult to check out the so-called divine qualities of a master or guru. But that can be a distraction as well.

Q: I also heard that some devotees have had spiritual experiences at the feet of their master, but these are difficult to evaluate because it is so subjective. But people who are around a master without being a devotee, let's say the taxi driver who drives the guru to the airport, don't feel anything special at all. Isn't that strange? It seems one only receives the blessing when one is open to their energy. If you would send a journalist from the BBC to make a movie about him, he will not feel anything if he is very critical about the guru. However, when I talk with these devotees, I got an idea of what is going on there. They say they feel so much love and peace when being about their master. That sounds very attractive to me.

JK: It may be a blessing and a curse. You may have great insights in a temple in India, Sri Lanka or Japan, but you could also get hooked to these experiences of joy, love and serenity. Now you are running after special experiences. And maybe you feel down when you must return home to your family and work. You are not able to appreciate 'normal' life anymore.

Q: But you haven't explained yet why there is no difference on the spiritual level between the seeker and the master. I can't believe that. I mean, I don't agree with you.

JK: Dualism only starts when the devotee believes that the master is on a higher level on the spiritual hierarchy. This is an additional form of labelling. This labelling originates from the belief that one wave is made of better water than another wave. One wave may be higher than another wave, but the essence is the same. The master may be a big wave and you may be a small wave. He has special powers and you do not. However, you are both made of water. That is nondualism. A lot of people are not very clear about this issue.

Q: What exactly do you mean?

JK: It means that although the differences are obvious, and although followers can learn so much from a master, or they can experience great moments of insight, love or delight while being with their master, yet they are sharing the same infinite awareness. The quality of the awareness is one and the same. The appearances are different of course, and it is not wrong to label these, but the core is one and the same. The waves are different in shape and size, but the essence is the same.

Q: Do you feel the need to discourage people to go and see such masters?

JK: No, not at all. Go and see them when you feel attracted to them. Check them out, if you want to study this phenomenon. Open your heart to them if you feel a natural desire to show devotion to a master. Even Nisargadatta, the famous master from Bombay, said that he showed devotion to his master, and that he followed his words because he trusted him. He said that meeting his master was crucial for his spiritual journey. And he showed even devotion after his master died. And yet, he was one of the most clear and uncompromising teachers of Advaita. So, I believe devotion is fine, it can be a way of showing respect and loyalty to someone who gave you so much clarity and who was a catalyst in rediscovering your inner stillness.

Q: What is a catalyst?

JK: In chemistry, a catalyst is a substance that increases the rate of a chemical reaction without itself undergoing any permanent chemical change. For example, ash acts as a catalyst in promoting the breakdown of sugar. When you hold a white sugar cube on top of a flame of a candle, it doesn't burn, it just turns dark. But when you add some ashes to the sugar, it will burn immediately. At the end of the process, the ashes are still there. The sugar is burned but the ashes remain untouched – although they were essential for the process to take place. The ash is the catalyst.

When Barack Obama delivered his Nobel Lecture in Oslo and brought a message of peace and hope, his words inspired millions of people. When the Dalai Lama speaks about compassion, he can inspire millions of people worldwide. Their words are a catalyst for a process of compassion, non-violence and peace. In a similar way, the guru in India can be a catalyst in being a mirror for the devotee. The master makes it possible that the seeker discovers that impersonal awareness within, which is also without. It might become clear that both 'share' this awareness. That there is one awareness which both guru and devotee are. Then there may appear resonance in the room.

Q: Yes, I know what you mean. You can also experience it with contemporary Advaita teachers. I have experienced resonance at several occasions. It is sometimes described as an energetic phenomenon.

JK: Then the separation between master and follower is gone. When the master points to that which both are, he or she is not changed by the conversation, and yet some recognition has taken place during the conversation. His words or his presence were a catalyst for the process of clarity and recognition.

Q: Is that what is called satsang? They say that in Hinduism, it means literally 'in the company with the truth'.

JK: Yes. But I am not an expert in Advaita. I prefer to talk about nondualism in simple terms. Even a twenty-year-old with no background in philosophy or spirituality should be able to follow what we are talking about here. Even someone who has not read any book about Zen or Advaita should be able to follow my words. I avoid religious and spiritual terminology as much as I can. I want to point to that which is the same in all religions, and which is also true for atheists. If we start to use specific terms, we are excluding those people who are not familiar with these words. I try to bring a message which doesn't exclude anyone.

Q: Why would people put a master on a higher level than themselves, while they know we all share the same awareness?

JK: There are many reasons to do so. I mentioned already respect and loyalty. Another one is avoidance. By putting the master on a higher level, you automatically put yourself lower. As a result, you can look up at the master and say to yourself, "The master has reached liberation, but I am not there yet. I will still need to do a lot of practice to reach the same level." So, in that way, the spiritual ego uses the labelling as a tool to postpone its own clarity.

What you *think* you are
is the person on the periphery
of the turning wheel,
apparently subject to the laws
of cause and effect.
What you *really* are is
the centre of the turning wheel,
which remains still and untouched.
And this centre also contains
the periphery of this wheel,
and even all the rest.

Don't Open that Door

Q: I know exactly what you are saying, I see what your nondual philosophy is pointing to. But still there is doubt arising here.

JK: Firstly, I would say, you can't *know* what I am pointing to. It is impossible to know, it is impossible for the mind to understand. Secondly, the sense of doubt is another trick of the mind. Let's see what doubt means. When you say there is doubt, it means that you are not sure about something. That is a thought which passes by. Why not be that which you are totally sure of? Is there anything you can say now without any doubt in your mind?

Q: Well, I can say that there is a world. I can say that life is happening. I can also claim without any doubt that I am.

JK: Ok. That's all we need for now. Just to be. Just the 'I am' is the beginning and the end of our exploration. Just to be. Simply presence. It is not an object or a person, it is just aware space.

Q: I experience a sense of resistance when you point to this space. If I go deeper into this stillness, my breathing seems to stop, and I am afraid that I would lose consciousness. It even feels like dying. I believe there is some resistance inside me against the emptiness of this space.

JK: Don't forget that the resistance doesn't come from the spaciousness but from the voices in your head. Don't listen to the turbulence created by the mind. These voices start to shout to each other, these parrots now push the buttons on your computer which release emotions (the orange button), they can even create physical sensations in your body (the red button). And your spiritual ego might get trapped by that. If that would be the case, don't fight it, let it happen. And then at some point, you might notice that these voices are only some parrots trying to distract you from unmasking the ego they are trying to defend. Just don't take it seriously.

Q: Ok, there is no need to worry about this. Even when I feel shortage of breath, headaches or panic.

JK: Don't identify with these dark clouds passing by. The space in which they appear remains unstained. This aware space *is* already the 'real' is-ness. There is nowhere to go to reach is-ness.

Q: I prefer a teaching where I can walk a path, step by step.

JK: I understand that. No need to get seduced now by a method or path which looks safer because then the spiritual ego is included in the game. The parrots will try to give you a task, so that the seeker can survive. By postponing the unmasking of the person, the parrots can keep on running their show. But parrots only repeat the words of others. They can't be trusted.

Q: I am also attracted to spiritual schools which have a lineage, which have strict rules of conduct, and a serious method to apply every day, with the perspective of getting the final goal after years of spiritual practice. I am thinking about, for example, the ancient Zen schools of Kyoto. Such old traditions are much more impressive to me than your dry Advaita. Or is it again my mind which is looking for new sensations?

JK: What if you don't need to achieve anything at all on the spiritual level? There are still the usual things you need to do on the human level, like brushing your teeth, getting dressed, making breakfast, driving to work, paying the bills, cooking dinner, looking after your family, taking care of your fellow people who need you, and so on. But on the spiritual level, there is no more homework. How do you feel about that? You know I must add here that the separation between the human level and the spiritual level is artificial, I only use it to explain this issue. But if we look at it, how could you ever make any effort to be stable in awareness or spaciousness? If you believe such an idea, you are trapped in the search because you will need a second concept to get rid of the first concept.

Q: How do you mean?

JK: It is all based on a misunderstanding. The voices in your head are taking over the business.

Q: The parrots in my mind are chattering and I can't control them.

JK: And they are lying to each other. You believe your own lies. Or you believe what others have told you. The first lie is the identification with personhood. You received your first name from your parents, but it is not what you really are. You believe the first lie and then you need a second lie to get rid of the first one. You look for a method to get rid of personhood. That method - which is going to bring you to liberation - is the second lie. Why not unmask both concepts right away? Why not put it all in the bin? First you believe in black magic which stops you from finding the truth, and then you look for a technique of white magic to get rid of the black magic. But the black magic was illusory. When that is clear and obvious, the need for the white magic falls away. In this analogy, both are magic, both are illusory. When this is clear, what is left? It is the single eye that sees all but this eye itself can't be seen. And it is what we are. Be that. Well, I don't have to give you the order to be that, because it was already being done anyway. I can't give you any homework.

Q: But these voices keep coming. I feel the pull towards spiritual exercises, I am fascinated by temples and gurus and incense.

JK: You can be fascinated by them, but you may also wonder if these are necessary to be what you are. I know that these voices and tendencies are vying for attention. These parrots are trying to seduce you. Why not ignore them? If you go into those issues with more questions, maybe you are only fueling your own beliefs. Just don't feed the thought "I need to be sure about this" or even "I have to do something to attain my true nature". And if the thoughts appear again, don't feed them. You are feeding those parrots by giving them fresh seeds every day.

Q: I must stop feeding the parrots in my head?

JK: It is not a task I give, it is again an attempt to make things clear. After this experiment, I will have to add that there is no 'you' who can ignore the parrots or feed the parrots. But during the experiment, just imagine for only two minutes that you are real and see what this experiment brings up. Recognize that these voices are trying to pull you back into personhood.

Q: These voices are experts in misleading each other. I need to have a closer look at them.

JK: I would say that such moments of insight usually don't feel as a task. They are rather accompanied with a smile, with laughter even, because you may realize that it was all so simple and obvious from the beginning, but it remained unnoticed.

Don't try to create an image
of aware beingness,
because then it will be limited
to a concept in your mind.

A Sense of Peace and Silence

Q: I have learned to become aware of the nature of thought. It took me years of practice. By taking the position of just being an observer of 'my' thoughts, by being a silent witness of images that come and go in my mind, I discovered that all thoughts are the same sort of noise. I could say that they are temporary appearances that come and go like clouds in the sky. I also learned not to judge my thoughts and feelings which pass by. I try to look at them as a neutral observer.

JK: Our minds have a natural tendency to give more importance to one thought over another. It is even stronger when emotions are involved. We can't beat that habit easily. But there is no need to attack your own natural tendencies. It is like our bodies which have a natural tendency to look for pleasure and to avoid pain. It is like a cat who resides on a warm place, even if that is on the hood of a car. So, trying to break these tendencies is not as easy as we usually believe.

Q: However, people who practice mindfulness meditation say that when they pay no attention to any thought, they remain as a witness of these thoughts. Then, the space between two thoughts becomes apparent. These moments are like windows through which one can see the empty space 'behind' that stream of thoughts and emotions. You see the blue sky between the clouds. When practicing this on a regular basis, our awareness becomes more open and our thoughts demand less attention.

JK: Thoughts are like clouds, temporary appearances in the sky with little substance. We usually apply the image of the clouds in the blue sky as a metaphor for the perception of our thoughts, feelings and sense perceptions. They all appear and disappear in a sky which remains untouched. It is a good metaphor, but like any metaphor it has its flaws.

Q: Clouds seem to appear out of nothingness, get a white or dark color, and then disappear again. No need to complain about the weather. And these clouds are perceived by naked awareness.

JK: These clouds are made of water. But the water isn't just in the clouds. The air around us is a gas which also contains water. When humidity is high, and you pour cold champagne in a glass, you will notice how the water of the air sticks to the glass. But most of the time we can't see the water in the air because the drops of water are too small to be noticed. In this analogy, nondualism recognizes the water everywhere, not just in the clouds. The waterdrops are both in the clouds as well as in the rest of the air.

Q: It is all one substance. It also became clear to me that our life story is mainly structured from thought. Our memory links these thoughts and emotions together in chains of meaning and that makes them important. And a lot of people live mainly in a conceptual world. I found that out through mindfulness meditation and yoga. Before, I used to be in my head all the time.

JK: By being in our heads, we create and confirm our life story. We got hypnotized into this movie from early childhood by our parents who were repeating again and again that we are a person residing in a body.

Q: How can we get rid of this identification?

JK: The one who wants to get rid of the identification is the one who seems to be standing in the way. How can the ego throw itself out? Can the ego fire herself from the only job it has? Does the ego even want that? Still, we can have a look at the mechanisms which created this hypnosis.

Q: A classic way to do so is to bring the person in the presence of the actuality. We should get rid of our compulsive thoughts first, otherwise we are to much in our heads and we can't focus on our awareness. For example, we can expose our habit of listening to our voices in our head by simply paying attention to them. Usually, one asks the person to focus on something else, simply to distract the mind. One asks the participant to become aware of his or her right hand. And then expand this sensation of physical presence to the rest of the body until it is one field of awareness. The entire body is now felt as one energy field. It feels good, and it is relaxing on a deeper level as well. It is also a method to slow down the thinking process for a few moments. This can also be done by focusing on breathing, or by focusing on the gap between two thoughts. This inner peace can also be achieved by bringing the attention to the position of the body, like in yoga or tai chi. Or by paying attention to the direct physical environment and the sensory experience of the actual moment. In this way, the trance-like habit of living constantly in our thoughts might be broken.

JK: All this sounds very interesting, especially as one also keeps in mind that the person who is doing these exercises is itself also a cloud passing by. In other words, your spiritual ego may kidnap this technique to turn it into a tool to reach a higher state in the future. You might say to yourself, "By practicing more, I will make myself more available for liberation." That was one of the parrots again. Notice this voice when it appears in your head. In nondualism, we remain vigilant about these subtle tricks of the spiritual ego.

Q: Yes, I understand. But that is not something we have learned in the mindfulness courses. In the mindfulness training it is still about the person, and how to get a better life. A more peaceful life. Which is fine. But I felt I had to go further. I noticed that my person was only a character in my movie. And now I am inviting other meditators in our group to see that our life story is like a movie which is played in front of our eyeballs.

JK: We might as well check it out right away. What exactly is the nature of the awareness which is observing the movie of our life? Is it one source or is it everywhere? Can the light of the movie theatre be found?

Q: You said it is an impersonal aware consciousness that perceives the movie. It is like a space in which the actors come and go without leaving a trace.

JK: Yes. We usually imagined that 'our' cognitive space is in our brain, but maybe it is rather a boundless space without any center. But this awareness is not an empty black box, it is both empty and full.

Q: And it seems to be aware of itself, it seems to be like a conscious awareness without anything to be *aware of*. But we don't notice this during everyday life because we are so distracted by what we see.

JK: When we close our eyes, we can easily notice at our eyelids that the light of the environment creates an orangey-grey field upon our closed eyelids because they are partly translucent. Can we find a perceiver of this colored field, a few centimeters behind each individual eye who is looking at each eyelid in front?

Q: We see one field for both eyes, not two fields for each eye. It is only one single orangey-grey field, there are not two separate fields for each eye.

JK: And where does the witnessing take place?

Q: Something behind the eyeballs? A certain area in the outer layer of the brain? Or maybe it is just one space. Front and back, the same spaciousness.

JK: If we put a hand in front of our eyelids, the orangey-grey field now turns into a black field. But is the space still there?

Q: Yes, it is still there. The spaciousness is still here. We are perceiving a dark space now instead of an orangey-grey one. It is a sort of colorless dark grey space in front of our eyes.

JK: Is this dark space limited in any direction?

Q: No.

JK: Can we find its borders?

Q: No. It is without borders, it is limitless.

JK: What happens if we take the hand away again, while we keep the eyes closed? The orangey-grey field is there again. But it is witnessed by and as the same space, it is only the color which turned brighter.

Q: Yes, it is the same space.

JK: And is there any distance between our 'me' and this witness?

Q: No.

JK: If no distance can be measured, it means that we *are* this aware knowing-being.

Q: This is what they call the impersonal knowingness. This aware space which has no boundaries, is what we really are. But there is no looker inside doing the witnessing of the orangey-grey field.

JK: And if we open our eyes, it is still the same impersonal witness! It is one same space for 'all of us'. If there is no border to be found, it is limitless. It is infinite. This immediateness and spaciousness is the closest we can get to describe this indescribable aware space which we are.

Q: Eyes open, eyes closed, the space remains untouched. However, when we open the eyes, we are watching the movie again.
And then the idea of being a person might appear again, for example, when someone else calls us by our name.

JK: Exactly. But that is the old habit again, which has practical value. The person apparently reappearing is not a problem.
But it doesn't mean that this person is also doing the witnessing. Notice how the ego wants to say, "I am doing it." This person only pops up from time to time, but it is not what we are.

Q: I see.

JK: After 'noticing' that there is an aware beingness witnessing our life through feelings, thoughts and sense perceptions, we can wonder if this awareness is present in all our experiences. Or is it sometimes switched off?
It will be hard to find a moment when it is switched off because the moment of such an absence would be seen 'through' and 'with' this same awareness.

Q: How simple!

JK: We can also wonder if there is any separation between this aware witnessing and the feelings, thoughts and sense perceptions which 'pass by' continuously.

Q: There is no delay. It is always fresh and immediate. And it feels good, peaceful.

JK: The natural fragrance of this space is peaceful and silent, and this becomes obvious when the chattering of the mind is absent.
But we didn't bring in the peace and silence, we didn't visualize this peace and silence. You don't need to burn incense for that to happen. It seems that it was already like that before we noticed it.

Q: Is this the state of presence I read about in the Advaita books? Is this the final state?

JK: No. No matter how great it feels, it is still perceived. Otherwise you wouldn't be able to tell me that it felt so good and peaceful. Even the state of presence, of pure 'I am' with no disturbing thoughts nor feelings nor perceptions, is still perceived. So even that can't be the final state, because this sense of pure 'I am' is still phenomenal. What we all share is the space in which even the subtlest experience or expression is witnessed. Even the sense of empty space is perceived.
And this may sound abstract, but it is closer than close. It is not an exclusive thing, nor a spiritual thing, it is the birthright of all of us.

We are all this, timelessly, no matter if it is recognized or not. Even when we are experiencing a lot of noise, the space is still here and everywhere.

The ultimate witness
it is not checking us out
from behind mirror glass.
It is the aware space
which doesn't exclude
anyone or anything.

Impersonal Space

Q: You say that this aware space – that which we really are – is not an individual property or a private territory but that it is *impersonal*.

JK: It can't be owned by someone. Nobody can claim it. This aware spaciousness is not bordered by our body or thoughts. It is literally that in which everything appears. In other words, this presence can contain everything. From the smallest emotion to the most distant star. So, we say it has no borders.

Q: It is infinite.

JK: And because it is infinite, it has no neighbors, so we can't have two or three of them. It's the one without a second. It is as simple as that. There is only one presence. And it's not something you can achieve after a long spiritual quest, it's what everybody is. If there is only one space, and this space has no boundaries, then nobody is excluded. Everybody *is* this single beingness. Nobody is expressing it better than anyone else. In other words, there are no hierarchies on the being level, the borders only become apparent in the mind on the human level. That which we all really are, knows no borders on the outside and no separation within.

Q: This means that we are all one.

JK: Yes, we are, but when you put it like that it sounds a bit like a quote on a new age postcard with a photograph of a sunset or so. This nondual oneness is very ordinary and not spiritual in any way.

Q: In nondualism, being one is obvious on the absolute level, while personhood is seen as conceptual.

JK: We all say 'I' all the time, so one could say we all have the same name. All actors are equal expressions of this ocean of beingness, despite their difference in appearance on the human level. All appear as images in and as this oneness. The world population could be described as one big starfish with almost 8 billion arms. One arm is not of a higher caste than any other arm. This makes nondualism very democratic. Nobody is inferior, nobody is superior, nobody is excluded. As beingness, we are all one, independent of our religion, color of skin or political background.

Q: Although we are all different at the level of the person, at the level of being we are all equal and the same.

JK: This being is the same naked is-ness we already were as a baby – and we still are that pure being. Although it may be less obvious that we still are that same pure being now because we are hypnotized by the story of the actor.

When you watch a movie, you don't see the white screen in the front and you don't see the white light in the back. But the essence – the light - is everywhere, whether it is recognized or not.

Q: And this essence is the same for everyone.

JK: Yes. Understanding that all human beings share this naked beingness, makes nondualism a good basis for tolerance and respect. To love one's neighbor as oneself is not a commandment we try to follow because we believe that it's something we ought to do. Hurting someone else is like stabbing your own ribs with a knife.

So being mild and compassionate towards others – friends and enemies - is like taking good care of yourself. It follows automatically as soon as there is the full understanding that the 'other' and 'yourself' are the very same 'we.' The other is just another expression of our true self. And the 'old need' of the ego to separate the others in enemies or friends loses its significance as well.

Q: The voices which separate people into groups, like different races, different countries, different languages, different religions, different political parties, these all lose their meaning in the light of nondual wisdom.

JK: These old parrots in your head don't receive any food any more. They might still try occasionally, but when 'you' stay clear and vigilant, they don't stand a chance any more.

We don't need to attain
anything special or spiritual
in order to be aware beingness.
We even don't need to
get rid of anything
to be what we really are.

The Dream

Q: Several authors of nondualism state that the idea of being a person is an illusion. Some masters from the East also state that the whole world is Maya, that it is all an illusion.

JK: The notion that we are separate human beings feels true on the human level, but in fact it is all conjured up in our mind. It is almost like a global self-hypnosis, and the difficulty with unmasking this hypnosis is that everybody agrees upon the reality of it. Some call it humanity's big daydream.

Q: Where does it come from?

JK: It is all a result of belief and hearsay. All we say and do is based on this hypnosis, which is built up by concepts about space, time and individuality. It's like a collective dream of humanity which is around for thousands of years. However, it's not necessary to attack this daytime dream, there is no need to try and prove it is all an illusion. We can, for example, know that it is an illusion but *pretend* that it is all real. It is no use to say it is all imagined, but we could also be open to the idea that there is a deeper reality which is common for all of us.

Q: How can we do that?

JK: If we take two minutes to let aside all our conditionings and then look 'within ourselves,' it may be seen that the *beingness* we all share – the naked awareness which we all are – has never been absent and never will. It is the one common denominator of all humanity.

Q: How can you know that for sure?

JK: I can't. It is not something which I can prove. But when this space is discovered in your own heart, in the center of your own being, and there is a taste for the vastness of it, it might become clear that this space has no boundaries. As a result, it may be obvious that it is also in the 'center' of the other human beings – whether they have recognized that or not. It doesn't matter that much whether these other beings are 'real' separate entities or only *imagined* separate beings.

Q: I have had an experience like that, a sense of unconditional love combined with a seeing that all separation is in the mind. From then on, I believe that I really 'know' what these masters are talking about.

JK: It is the most obvious and yet the most overlooked thing there is. But 'it' isn't a thing of course, it is not an object, it's not a sensation, it can't be seen or felt or heard, and yet it is the origin of all our thoughts, feelings and perceptions. And it is not residing in a center inside your body, it is borderless. It is the space in which everything can come and go. It is also space for humanity's big daydream.

Q: I see.

JK: In several spiritual circles, the person is often regarded as a thing to get rid of. But when the person can be observed by aware beingness, the sense of personhood is reduced to its real proportions. It is one of the ten thousand things. Instead of fighting against it, it can be celebrated. And this is as much true for 'your own' personality as for the 'other ones'.

What if we would be able
to notice that the awareness
which looks through our eyes
at 'other' people
is the same awareness
which looks through
our fellow people at us?
What if this is just
one single aware space?

Who Am I?

Q: How would you define our true nature, and how can we recognize it and feel it in our heart?

JK: Let's first find out what we mean by our true nature. When we look for our identity, are we content with something which changes its identity on a regular basis, or are we going to look for something which never changes? The person we believe to be is not as stable and permanent as we believe. Only our memory makes a stable image of our body and mind.

Q: How do you mean?

JK: First we can notice that most of the time we are not actively aware to be a person. Our attention is simply with the present moment, which could be a sense of thirst, the sense of sitting on a chair, a sensation of joy or pain, and so on. Or our attention is simply with perceiving the meaning of these words. Thousands of different images pass by like that, each day. But only a few of them are images which clearly refer to our identity as a person.
Secondly, the ego can change its mask several times a day. The ego has many masks. Even in one day we can play the role of child or parent, brother or sister, seeker or teacher, employer or employee, neighbour or colleague, friend or enemy. We automatically shift from one role into the next one, and we talk and

114

behave accordingly. We can play many roles with our body, but who or what is behind all these different roles we play? What is the nakedness behind all these masks? And what is observing all these roles we play?

Q: It is not easy to answer this question.

JK: There is no need to give a smart answer, there is absolutely no need to give me a mental answer. Don't rely on your memory. It has no value if we repeat the words from a book we have read. Instead of trying to give an intellectual answer, just stay with the question, and notice that there is a space which allows these questions and answers to appear.

Q: We need to let the question sink into our heart, so that we give an answer which is not just intellectual but also digested and felt?

JK: Right. An intellectual understanding is important as well, but it's not enough. We are not referring to a space which is out there and which you can reach during meditation or while practicing yoga. We *are* that space. There is no distance between us and the spaciousness.

Q: So, who or what is observing all these roles we play during the day?

JK: If we allow this question to sink in, it is as if we are standing in front of a mirror, and we wonder if that reflection of that face at one meter away is what we really are. What is the real witness of these observations? What is observing the reflection of the mirror and what is also observing the perceptions in our body and our thoughts and feelings? Where is that one to be found? Can it be identified at all? Do we even need to identify that witness?

Q: I can't answer the question and yet that space feels very familiar.

JK: Yes, this spaciousness feels very familiar and is closer than close. Much closer than all the roles we play during the day. It is also more stable than the roles in 'our' story. These words will also pass, but this aware space will not pass. It was already here before we talked about it. What can we say about this spaciousness, if anything?

Q: Not much. I would say it is something very light and transparent.

JK: Does it have a form? Does it have a specific colour?

Q: No.

JK: Is it growing old? Can it become ill? Does this spaciousness run after a certain goal? Does it have a task to fulfil? Is it related to a specific religion?

Q: No.

JK: It watches our thoughts and feelings come and go, but it itself cannot come and go. It witnesses time and space, but it's not affected by time or space. It allows everything to happen, but it is not participating in the story. It is the stage on which the opera is played, but the stage will remain untouched when the opera is over. What name could we give to this invisible stage? What kind of qualities could we give to the aware space which allows all qualities to appear and disappear? Can this final perceiver, which even perceives identity, time and space, be located? And where exactly are 'we' in all this? Can we be separated from this space?

Q: How can we know if this witness is really the impersonal witness? How can we know it is not just the ego *pretending* to be the final witness?

JK: We can check it out. If the ego puts on the mask of witness, it will still have some interest in what is happening in our story. It is still involved, although maybe very subtly. The parrots may start talking again. And the parrots get smarter over the years, they even talk nondual language now. The spiritual seeker has many tricks to pretend to be the final

117

witness. The seeker can even say that there is nobody, and that there is no me, no others, no space, just nothing. But the ego always betrays itself by showing some interest in what is happening on the screen. There is still some personal bias. The *real* final witness is not capable of being biased.

Q: Why is that?

JK: The final witness is not only witnessing 'your' movie, but it is also witnessing 8 billion other movies. So how could it be involved in some detail in one of those 8 billion movies? This light is not only shining in your movie or my movie, but in all these billions of movies at the same time.

The content of awareness
seems to overshadow
the pure awareness itself,
in the same way as
drawings and text balloons
grasp the readers' attention.
As a result, the white page
is completely overlooked,
while the reader of the cartoon
is staring at that white page.

The Perfection of Imperfection

Q: In nondualism, they say that there is no spiritual path. I find that extremely hard to accept.

JK: What we are looking for *is* already fully available. This means that we don't need to create anything new, we don't need to make any effort. Our mind says there must be evolution from the actual state which we label as 'so and so' to a future state which is (almost) perfect. But if past and future are concepts in our minds, then any form of evolution is also in our minds. That is why some teachers say that there is nowhere to go. And that is correct.

Q: I see. But how do we recognize this?

JK: There is no technique that can bring you to where you already are. If I would say to you, stand up from your chair, and I give you maximum three steps to go to your true nature, what would you do? Every step you take would be a step away from where you are, and yet, every step away is also where you are. It's a paradox. There is no escape. The 'I am' is always here, it is never absent. It is never elsewhere. It is never in the future. But this 'I am' is not personal. Don't let the ego kidnap the 'I am'.

Q: The ego only creates a sense of claustrophobia in the awareness by limiting itself to a cage of the body and mind.

JK: The sense of personhood is a concept which is added on top of the 'I am' and this mask *seems* to cover the original 'I am'.

Q: Your words are very inspiring to me. But how can I use your words to get the full effect for me?

JK: You can't use my words, like you would use an insight from a philosopher or a scientist. These words are only pointers to something I can't describe. They arise in spaciousness and point to spaciousness. Isn't it a paradox? They act as mirrors and that which is mirrored is a space with no borders. How many mirrors do you need for that? But my words themselves do not have any power on their own. And they don't serve you as a person either. Don't look for an effect for your 'me' because that will be temporary. And it will never be perfect in the eyes of your mind.

Q: But that perfection is exactly what most seekers want to attain.

JK: You as a person will not reach any goal when applying my words into daily life. The mind might use another trick, like whispering that you should become perfect, but you won't reach perfection as a person. Don't pay attention to that sneaky voice. The only perfection one may notice is the perfection of imperfection. But even saying it is perfect, is obsolete. It is as it is. No labels are necessary.

Q: I see. But if seekers are complaining or lamenting about their own life or about the troubles in the world, some sages might provoke them by saying that it is already perfect as it is.

JK: These sages don't ignore the misery and the problems in the world, they simply see the bigger picture. They see that left and right are always in a perfect balance. They see the balance within the imperfection. But that doesn't mean that the world will be perfect in the eyes of the human mind.

In the middle of the night,
the white light of a full moon
can be quite impressive.
But during the day,
That same moon light
is hardly recognizable.

What's wrong with the world today?

Q: I am very worried about how human beings are destroying nature over the last two centuries. The pollution in the air, the destruction of the rain forests, plastic in the oceans, the way we treat animals for consumption, climate change because of industrial activities, you know what I mean. I feel a need to save the world before it is too late. We need to think about the future generations. How does nondualism look at this?

JK: We can look at this issue from a being point of view and from a human point of view. From the being point of view, let's say the viewpoint of naked spaciousness, all the disasters you described are part of a greater unicity. In that sense, nondualism isn't designed to change the world.

But from a *human* point of view, we notice that our planet is ill and that it needs treatment. If the planet would be one of my patients, I would declare it as seriously ill. My conclusion as a doctor would be that medical care is needed right away. But I would also say that it is not the result of a few bad guys who are the usual suspects, such as a few politicians and a few bosses of certain multinationals, but that we are all in this.

Q: How do you mean?

JK: It is true that since the industrial evolution, we have achieved enormous progress on many levels, especially in the field of technology and comfort. We have houses, trains, cars, modern medical techniques like surgery, and so forth. I am very happy that we can have modern medical care when we need it. In that sense I am glad I am not living in the middle ages. But we also must deal with the down side. Medical techniques gave us new possibilities, but there are also the side effects of medication and the complications of technical medical procedures.

Q: This confirms the law of opposites, which says that each positive pole needs a negative pole. And that both are in balance anyway. The Chinese Taoist's said centuries ago that everything has a shadow side.

JK: We postulate the same theory in nondualism.

Q: But why are human beings treating their planet in such a bad and irresponsible way? Is it because we have lost contact with nature?

JK: Those who live in a big city obviously lost contact with nature because everything is provided by modern society. We don't have to go and hunt if we are hungry. We buy our food in the supermarket without knowing where it comes from. Most people have no clue how it was made, and they are not even questioning this. We lost sight of the laws of nature, we eat processed food, and we live inside houses or offices with heating and cooling. We don't need to go to the river or lake to get fresh water. Because of this evolution over the last centuries, we seem to be far away from the people in ancient times who were more subject to the dangers and discomfort of wild nature. But on the other hand, they had no pollution, no traffic jam, no invoices to pay.

Q: When the native people in South America were living deep in the forest, they tried to do this with respect towards life and in harmony with nature. When today's businessmen walk in the Amazon, they don't see birds and insects, but they see a business opportunity. They don't mind about the consequences for the environment or for the local people, they are only focussed on their own profits. Isn't that also because they have forgotten their inner true self? Isn't that what yoga and mindfulness meditation are pointing at? We have closed our hearts because we live mainly in our heads. Our lives have become completely ego driven.

JK: Most people of civilised countries have additionally lost touch with reality and with nature because they are more in their heads than in their sense perceptions. They don't see and hear what is on display in the moment because their head is filled with thoughts about past and future. They are more into concepts, beliefs and expectations and overlook the ever freshness of what is. They miss the aliveness of the mountain river by giving the river a name. One of the reasons is our ability to think in concepts. Human beings can think in abstract terms. This power has brought us many achievements, but we have taken the words, the symbols and the concepts for the real world. As the Buddhists say, modern man is lost in thought and as a result has lost the world. A lot of people have lost the basic sense of compassion and respect for other living beings. In that sense, we can learn a lot from Buddhist teachers.

Q: And we compensate this loss by looking for happiness or satisfaction in the outside world of things, such as success and power. We defend our territory, and want to make it bigger if we can. It is all egocentric behaviour. As a result, we look for happiness in a position in society, in a bank account or in material wealth -- rather than in tangible wealth such as authentic relationships or enjoying nature as it is. I believe mindfulness meditation is a good way to become aware of this. I am more aware of the present moment now. I listen less to the inner voices in my head than before I practiced mindfulness meditation.

JK: We also let the aliveness of the present moment pass by because we need to take a photograph and then post it on the social media. Apparently, that is more important for us than being present in the moment.

Q: The problem is obvious when one sees people staring at their smartphone with their chin down - while sitting with friends in a restaurant.

JK: And if it isn't the smartphone or the photograph which overshadows the present moment, it is equally disturbed by our stream of thoughts. It is amazing how much our attention is in thought and, as a result, we feel disconnected with the actual reality. The subtitles in our movie are so big that they are overshadowing our sense perceptions.

Q: We don't notice the white screen any more.

JK: As a result, our actual sense perceptions are sometimes completely overlooked. We walk on the beach but don't hear the surf because we listen to the inner voice which complains about the troubles at work from last week. We are lying in a warm bath and are frustrated about an important business meeting we will have in two days. We are drinking a great wine, but we miss out the perfume, taste and after taste of the wine because we are having an argument about international politics with our friend who sits in front of us.

Q: And as humanity seems to confuse the real world of pure nature with mere signs and symbols, such as bank balances, newspaper articles, religious rules, political ideas, business contracts, we are destroying nature. Company owners don't see the trees of the rainforest, but they see a business opportunity. They see dollars instead of trees.

JK: It sometimes seems that we are so tied up in our minds that we have 'lost' our sense perceptions, or should we say, that we lost our senses. And we identify not only with our own egocentric projections, we also have collective dreams and ideas. It may be on a small scale like a football team or on a larger scale like a country. I always thought it was a bit odd if people were proud about their nation. I thought that being proud was justified when you achieved something because of your talents or hard work. Like one can be proud about winning a local tennis championship, climbing a mountain, running your first marathon or getting a new job. But if you say you are proud to be an American, you haven't done anything to achieve that, it is just a description on your passport. You have no reason to take credit for it. But you will walk around with your flag, being proud about that country. And soon you will meet someone who says, "I am proud to be Russian." And when two different flags meet, a territorial conflict is never far away. And both of you are willing to sacrifice your lives for a flag. I believe the ego just loves to stand out, it likes to look for conflict to confirm itself. We all have some sense of territory inside us.

Q: We also notice this behaviour when looking at the animal world. They defend their territories as well.

JK: Yes, the sense of territory is deeply rooted in the genes of animals as well. But humans add an additional layer on top of that. Our minds put an extra world on top of the real world. A purely conceptual world. And we believe that the symbols represent reality. As if the map is the land. And we draw a line on the map and we claim that land as ours. And we have wars on that, one flag attacking another flag because the colours and stripes are slightly different. We start huge conflicts based on concepts, because the language is different, because the colour of the skin is different, because the belief in a holy book is different. We should realize that the symbol is secondary, it doesn't have the same value as the original reality it is referring to.

Q: Where does nondualism come into all this?

JK: I believe that nondualism points out several mechanisms of human behaviour which are at the origin of all these problems you were referring to. Apart from natural disasters like tornados, tsunami's and earthquakes, many of the problems of the world are man-made. Or should I say, mind-made? Even before the industrial revolution, humans were fighting each other for symbols and ideas.

Q: And it only got worse since. But how could nondualism ever be of any value here?

JK: The short answer is that nondualism can't solve the problems of the world. And it has no intention of doing so because it sees things as they are - without labelling.

Q: But as a sort of side effect of the nondual wisdom, our human part could become more concerned and we become more compassionate.

JK: Yes, that's very likely, but there are no strict rules.

Q: But I must say that my 'nondual understanding' made me aware that most of our conflicts are based on the ego. And nondualism is one of the most direct ways of pointing out that this ego is also a concept. In that sense, it is even more direct than Buddhism.

JK: It is interesting to see how the need to label everyone is just a habit of the mind. Our sense of personhood is in our minds. If one has understood the basics of nondualism, it will be hard to walk around with a flag and kill other people because they defend another flag. You know that everybody is the same single awareness, so where would you find inspiration and motivation to attack other people? You no longer think in terms of high and low, so where would you find inspiration to look down on other people? You simply don't get seduced into these mind games any more.

Q: Seeing that life is nondual by nature may be a big relief for many people. All these mind games would lose their impact. If everybody would realize his or her true nature, if everybody would taste the sense of compassion which Buddhism describes, we would have a different world, isn't it? So, in that sense, nondualism could contribute largely to this change we need so much.

JK: Yes, theoretically that is true. But people won't listen to you if you come with such a nondual message. The voices of their ego are more powerful than you imagine. This nondual wisdom is not attractive at all for the mind. The voices of their ego will prevent them from even listening to a conversation like this. They still hold on their territory, their religion, their ideas. Yet, I will not stop you from your intention to create a better world. If that is what your human part is designed to do, I respect that totally. But you might also check whether your 'good' intentions are also ego based in a subtle way.

Q: Maybe they are ego driven, because I consider myself as one of the good guys and those corrupt politicians and greedy businessmen obviously as the bad guys. I realize just now that this is another form of dualism. I started form the assumption, 'I am better than they are.' And I confirm this by fighting against the bad guys. Fighting against evil is also based on judgement. And the war against evil is another war. Maybe that is why Buddhists have integrated this deeper wisdom and seem to avoid any conflict.

JK: And yet, if you feel like doing something about these issues, why not? The sickness of the planet really needs treatment. Let us be clear about that.

Q: Thank you.

JK: You may also take a step 'backwards' and look at this world from the sense of awareness instead of the sense of personhood. Maybe we can see the balance in the apparent chaos. Maybe we notice that despite all the troubles, despite the dark side of the planet, there is also a bright side. And maybe, as the Chinese said, both are always in balance.

Nondual freedom is not about
someone being free but
freedom from someone-ness.

What is Our Original Identity?

Q: In nondualism, they say that our original identity is the key to freedom. What do they mean with our original nature? It sounds a bit abstract to me.

JK: The original nature refers to that naked being or is-ness which was already here before we were born. Zen Buddhists describe it as 'Our Original Face.' It also refers to the spaciousness which will still be there after our body dies.

Q: How can we find this out?

JK: We can believe the ancient scriptures, that is the easy way. We just accept what our priests have told us, and we follow the rules of our community. Or if we are more sceptic by nature, we try to see for ourselves. And the questions are more important than the answers. What is your original identity, before you received a name from your parents? What is your original being, before you learned to identify with your body and mind? And is this original being still here?

Q: My mind gets stuck when I try to answer these questions.

JK: I know. The mind has no hold on this space. It is like a wave which tries to catch the ocean. It's not going to work. And yet, both the wave and the ocean are made of the same water. Their essence is one and the same. That is the key to answer the question.

Q: If I can find my wetness inside myself, I have the key to discover the common quality of both waves and ocean. What are the qualities of this spaciousness?

JK: A wave can't know wetness. A wave can't see the ocean in its totality. It is impossible to describe it because it is bigger than ourselves. If we would compare our individual body and mind with a balloon filled with air, there would be almost 8 billion small balloons floating in this space. The pure awareness could be compared with a huge balloon within which all these small balloons are floating. Of course, I must add here that this metaphor has several limitations. The big balloon is so big that it can't be measured. It is impossible to find its edges, that is why it is said to be infinite. We also cannot describe the big balloon because 'we' are residing in the middle of it and the small balloons are not capable of stepping outside the big balloon to have a proper look at the big one and then describe it in detail.

Q: So, we are stuck.

JK: And yet, at the same time, the air inside our little balloons is the same air as the air which fills the big balloon. That is why it is said that when we look in our heart, when we dive into our core, we discover the substance of both the small balloons and the big balloon.

Q: And where do these balloons come from? Where do they go to?

JK: These are typical questions coming from the mind. The ego wants to know why and how. These questions are only tricks of the spiritual ego to survive. It's a distraction. The seeker can only think in terms of past and future, in terms of cause and result, but the big balloon has never heard of time or causality. It even doesn't know about here or there. It just *is*. It can't even hear or speak. It is deaf and mute. It just is everything and everyone. It doesn't want to improve anything because it knows no high or low. It doesn't go anywhere because it is already everywhere.

Q: So, the big balloon, the infinite awareness, is not subject to evolution?

JK: Everything seems to be subject to time, but this spaciousness is not affected by time at all. It is beyond time. It is before time. It is timeless.

Q: So, we can't say where this big balloon is residing?

JK: Everything seems to be in a certain location, but this spaciousness is before any concept of location, beyond any frame of reference. You won't find it on your GPS. Trying to locate the big balloon is pointless. Your parrots inside your head are trying to seduce you with smart questions, but such conversations only distract you from the true questions.

Q: I see.

JK: But it is interesting to check if there is any distance between you and this space. If there is no physical distance, can you still say it is *different* from you? That is why it is said that what you really are is this limitless awareness.

Q: In other words, this spaciousness is what we really are. The person is what we *think* we are and is only a smaller part of the big awareness.

JK: If we don't hold to any idea about who we are, if we let go all the concepts or definitions we have about ourselves, all this is obvious. And what is also amazing is that we don't need to make any effort at all to be this space. We don't need to behave in a certain way to be worthy for this, we don't have to use visualization techniques to create this spaciousness. It's already fully here and now, no matter if we recognize this or not.

Thoughts are like clouds.
Some are white,
others are dark grey.
No need to chase
the dark clouds away.
No need to run after
the white clouds.
They are both
concepts passing by.

It is Fake News

Q: As a seeker, I made the classic mistake of comparing my inner state of confusion and doubt to another people's level on the spiritual path. The outer image I have of spiritual masters is that they are always in peace and joy, and that they radiate unconditional love. I have had tastes of bliss and love as well, but it never lasted very long. I tried to reach that state of perfection and permanence as well, I even tried to imitate certain behavior, hoping that this would help me in overcoming my imperfection. I was hoping to leave the large group of seekers and join the special club of finders. It took me several years before I realized that coming home is not about comparing your own state with someone else's state. I read about that in your book *Nobody Home*. I was tired of finding myself deficient. I did not feel deficient as a human ego because my life on a personal level and on a professional level was all fine, I had no financial or relational problems so to speak, but as a spiritual ego I felt like a failure.

JK: You listened to the voices which say you should be perfect on the spiritual level. And you seemed to believe these voices. Then, frustration is unavoidable.

Q: I will not make such a mistake again.

JK: That was such a voice again. These parrots are like agents who represent and defend the spiritual ego. None of our mistakes are really mistakes. And remember, these failures never touch who we really are, none of the labels you give yourself - or labels which others give to you - can stain the indestructible awareness which we all are and share.

Q: I believe that the egos of spiritual seekers can be very self-critical because we have the most exalted examples to compare ourselves to—like all the famous yogis and the great Buddhist masters.

JK: We forget that awakening to our essential nature has nothing to do with perfection but with clarity. It is not a matter of avoiding life or creating a perfect life. It has everything to do with seeing life just as it is.

Q: I see.

JK: It is all a matter of perspective, it is all a matter of how you look at things. When you look at things as a person, then there is left and right and good and bad, and that's fine. But when there is a looking *from* and *as* beingness, all this is put in perspective. Then there is simple the 'what is.' All that effort to reach the unattainable is not needed.

Q: I believe what you say, but it sounds still theoretic and abstract to me. Most spiritual paths are difficult, and only a few seem to reach the final goal. But you make it sound like it is easy and attainable by everyone. Can you introduce me into this effortlessness in a more direct way?

JK: Notice that you don't need to make any effort or go anywhere else to notice the natural sense of being here. Just simply being aware of being here. Why not bring your attention to this sense of being? Just the sense of presence. And one of the things which may happen is that in this space of being, the sense of personhood melts away. We don't need to chase it away, we don't need to attack it or make it smaller, it just doesn't show up.

Q: I see. But I sense an uneasiness coming up when I melt away into this void.

JK: While we are letting our attention being attracted to this natural sense of presence, the ego may start to panic because it notices that its favorite territory – what it describes as your personal life story – has been taken over by something it can't get its hands on. So, the ego will use all its tools to get its territory back. For example, it will wake up its parrots which will start to talk to each other like crazy. They are very well trained in this, and they excite one another by talking to each other. And this inner debate usually leads to an internal chatter, which mainly supports the belief that you are a person locked up in a body, a person with a past and a future, a person with characteristics, plans and obligations.

Q: And the parrots don't care if you are successful or unsuccessful. What matters to them is that you keep on believing that the person is real and solid.

JK: For example, if they notice you can't reach your goals in life, they will use that sense of failure to confirm your sense of personhood. The voices will say how *you* failed. And when they notice you have reached your goals in life, they will also use that sense of success to confirm your sense of personhood. They will tell you how good *you* are. The egocentric voices will always try to make it personal. And when talking is not enough, they will use their secret weapons. They will push the button of feelings and emotions, like feeling unworthy or self-satisfied, guilty or proud, happy or unhappy, strong or weak. They can even push the button of physical reactions in the body, and you will feel pain, dizziness or ecstasy. These voices walk on the scene without being invited, they just appear and start talking. This may lead to a sense of having to attack these voices, but that's not necessary.

Q: I can recognize that in my own case I was also attacked by these parrots in my head.

JK: However, some of these voices are whispering that the sense of space is what we really are, and the sense of personhood is only a tool to be able to function in society.

Q: So, there are some 'good' voices as well? Should I listen more to these ones? Are these whispering voices the ones I hear when I am away from society and its rules and expectations? Are these the tiny inner voices which talk to me after I walked in the park in silence or when I did a yoga session? During such moments, what you just said makes total sense. However, when I am in the middle of the game of life, the egocentric parrots are shouting again. What can I do about this?

JK: You know that in the end I can't give you any instructions or prescriptions. We are just playing a bit now, to explain how things work. There are no parrots in your head, no egocentric parrots and no 'good' voices. It's only a metaphor. In a way, it is too simple to put this into words. I have no magic key to open the door into this space because you are already 'it.'

Q: But I don't *feel* that way. I don't feel the peace, stillness and contentment. But I know it is possible to feel peaceful because I have experienced that silence for myself. It is frustrating. I even tried to do nothing, but I realized that this was just another doing, another trick of my ego who always wants to do something to get somewhere else in the future. I feel more like a human doing than a human being.

Sometimes I am so mixed up that I can't even sit in silence for ten minutes.

JK: Why not just stay in the noticing, in the witnessing, without following any thoughts? Just be.

Q: And the space is just here, right?

JK: And your sense of being here and your natural sense of space are not separated.

Q: Interesting.

JK: Physical experiences will continue to appear, pleasant sensations as well as unpleasant ones. See them, don't ignore them, don't connect with them. Just notice them come and go, without trying to manipulate them. Just observe, without direct interest. No need to analyze them or look for a treatment. All such thoughts would be confirming the story of the me, while here we would like to focus on this spaciousness in which all these thoughts and emotions are coming and going. And this spaciousness doesn't know any sense of lack, it is complete by itself as itself. It doesn't need past or future, it even doesn't know the present moment. And yet, there is a clear sense of presence, but not a person being present, just naked presence.

Q: Yes.

JK: And this spaciousness is not stained by the images that appear. Where does it begin, where does it end? No need to use imagination or memory. No need to label this as high or as spiritual. It is neutral and yet full of life. No need to trust or believe or expect. No need to go elsewhere to discover this awareness. No need to change your behavior to be this space. No need for a me. This awareness is effortless and never absent. It is said that this is what we are. But don't believe that. It is before any belief or physical experience. The spaciousness is not saying 'I am.' And if the sense of personhood would appear, it is another image on the screen.

Q: We are this.

JK: Yes, but you can't say that *you* are this, you can't claim it, and yet 'this' is what we all are. We have never been anything else than this, so trying to stay like this is meaningless. Some parrots in your head will try again to seduce you. Just stay as 'you' are. Effortlessly. Nobody is excluded from this. Even if you would be in deep meditation and full of bliss and peace, and suddenly you feel disturbed by someone calling you on your cell phone, this space is not gone. A voice in your head may suggest that you've lost it, but that is not true. Don't buy that. It is fake news. Such voices can't be trusted.

This unbreakable light of awareness
shines timelessly and effortlessly.
It absolutely doesn't need
our comments or improvements.

The Conflicts Between Super Ego's

Q: Why is there so much suffering in the world, and why do we keep on repeating the same mistakes?

JK: Many fights are based on conflicts between two egos who share a mutual territory. This may lead to a fight between two brothers who are sitting in the backseat of the car of their father, between two partners in a relationship, between two colleagues at work. Usually the fights are short-lived but sometimes such situations lead to a long-term conflict with recurrent suffering or even physical violence. Most conflicts are based on the tools of the ego, like identification, time and labelling.

Q: Yes, I agree, that is how nondualism looks at conflicts between two people. Hate, anger and revenge are all based on the ego. But my question was rather referring to the bigger conflicts on the planet.

JK: The same mechanisms apply, but simply on a larger scale.

Q: I see. It is again based on the identification with the ego, the need to label others as good or bad, and memory which recalls what others did to you in the past.

JK: When we read a newspaper, we notice a lot of conflicts in the world. When the habit of separating and labelling on the individual level now also is applied on a larger scale, we get a group of ego's, like in street gangs. When these must share territory, bigger conflicts are lurking around the corner.

When the same sense of separation and labelling is applied on even a larger scale, we get super ego's. A so-called super ego is a group of persons who have, for example, the same political idea about what is right and what is wrong, and they all feel very strongly about that. Sometimes they also have a charismatic leader who is an example for their identity. And they create a sense of additional power and importance by joining one another, and by avoiding a dialogue with those who have a different point of view. The larger the group, the more power. Each individual ego feels supported and confirmed by the group. These super egos confirm their identity with colors and flags and slogans. And when they meet a group with different ideas, with different flags, or when their territory is shared with another super ego, a super conflict is very likely to happen. It leads to a civil war, a religious war or even a world war.

Q: This mechanism has been at the core of conflicts for centuries.

JK: When this is applied on the level of sports, this is rather fun and maybe a healthy way to ventilate the need of human beings to defend their territory and the male desire to fight rivals. If one country fights another country during the Olympic Games, all this is fine. But when these mechanisms are applied in the real world, serious conflicts are almost inevitable. But super ego's do not only lead to bad things such as conflict and war.

Q: It can also have positive effects?

JK: Of course, no black without white. All these mechanisms can also work in the opposite way, but these forces don't receive as much attention in the media. Some individuals dedicate their lives to helping their fellow people. And when they join forces, the benefits for society are larger as well.

Q: I see. But they are not on the eight o'clock news.

JK: Look at great leaders such as the Dalai Lama, Gandhi or Nelson Mandela. They have pointed to compassion, non-violence and mutual understanding. They always tried to find a solution without conflict, without labelling other groups of people in a certain way. Such leaders point to what all beings have in common instead of emphasizing what is different between groups of people. We have lots of organizations which take care of the human condition without creating any additional violence or territory conflicts. They can appear on different levels, like families, local communities, national organizations and international clusters of people with similar ideas such as NGO's and other organizations.

Q: But despite all the good intentions of these NGO's, the results are not very impressive. Why is that? Is the greed and the dark side of humanity stronger than its counterpart?

JK: In nondualism, we are aware of all these conflicts in the world. We also notice that fighting against the bad guys is another fight, and that in some cases the initiative starts from labelling a certain group of people as bad. And this is another form of dualism. And such an approach usually doesn't work as well as the approach of non-labelling.

Q: We realize that we can't always fight these conflicts, because fighting against war would be a new war.

JK: What we can do is focus on that which we have in common instead of focusing on that which is different. And that is exactly what nondualism is about.

Q: How do you mean?

JK: If we look at the human body, we could say that most of our anatomy is the same. If we look at hands, all of them are made of the same bones, tendons, blood vessels, muscles, and so on. And yet, at the same time, not two hands are identical. This 'diversity within unicity' is a typical quality of how the human body is built. I made a series of photographs on this topic, illustrating this concept in a visual way instead of by pointing to it with books or lectures.

Q: I can see that there is diversity within unicity when looking at hands. And I am sure that this is also true for the rest of the body.

JK: All humans are built the same way, we all have a heart and lungs and kidneys and muscles and bones, and yet there are no two identical human beings on this planet. You don't have to be a doctor to notice that. So, in that sense, we have a lot in common. But the mind focusses on the differences, that is what our mind is good at.

Q: We notice immediately changes and differences. And these tiny differences are blown up. These are the bad parrots again, who point out the differences and ignore the common ground.

JK: All this labelling can lead to different groups, to different hierarchies. Some conflicts are based on physical differences like gender, physiognomy or color of the skin. Some are based on intelligence, language and culture. But most of the conflicts originate from purely conceptual differences, like religious or political differences. We zoom in on the 10% while at the same time more than 90% of what we are is identical. That is an illustration how mixed up the human mind is. When one observes carefully the inside of a human body, like during surgery, there is no difference between an American and a Russian patient, no difference between a Christian and a Muslim.

Q: You also made a series of photographs on that topic, isn't it?

JK: Yes. The subject of that series only wants to illustrate how we are all the same – literally - deep inside our bodies.

Q: In nondualism, you are not supposed to label anyone, which means that you are not allowed to criticize the bad guys. But you can point out the *common* field which both the good guys and the bad guys share. From the nondual point of view, the bigger picture is always kept in mind, right? You avoid zooming in on the small details which are different, like difference in gender or skin color or religious symbols. And you also make clear that this ego we all cherish so much, is way overrated.

JK: Yes, the ego is way overrated, it is given so much attention in society. If this ego can be unmasked as merely a concept, there is less need to defend this ego on a small scale. And it is very likely that the need to identify with a super ego also lessens. When people would be able to recognize that common ground, say the 90%, maybe their mind set would change. They would look through a wide lens instead of a tele lens.

Q: But nondualism is not trying to change the world, because that would mean we would need to attain a certain goal in the future, while that very future is also a concept.

JK: And the ego is not always the bad guy. Egos can do great things as well.

Q: And in nondualism it is also seen that everything is always in balance.

JK: Nondualism points to the perfection of this imperfect world. It points to that which is timeless. It points to what we have in common. And there is even no need to call it perfect or balanced. These words are only used in conversations like this, when we try to explain the presence of our common ground.

Q: You are pointing to the core of all of us.

JK: And it is not an abstract theory. When we are looking through our own eyes into someone else's eyes, we can notice that 'our' awareness which is looking at them is the same awareness which is looking from their eyes towards us. Isn't that an amazing discovery? So, we could say that this impersonal awareness is the light which shines in every human being. So, the need to identify with the personal sense of self can still be there, but it is just a temporary mask. And as a result, the need to identify with a super mask would become almost obsolete.

Q: If more people on the planet would see this, a world with less conflict would be a natural side-effect of nondual wisdom.

JK: And this question will not appear as soon as the person is absorbed in presence.

This space is so open
that it allows both
conflicts and peace.

The Voices of Ego are Addicted to Labelling

Q: You said that we are addicted to labelling.

JK: Yes, our minds are addicted to labelling. And we hardly realize that. We see someone's face, even the face of a stranger in the subway, and immediately the mind gives comments, both in the positive way or the negative way. We apply this to our fellow human beings as well as to ourselves. And we are also wondering what others think about us. So, some of us live as if they are defined by the labels of other people.

All this takes a lot of energy. We need to polish our mask every day. But in fact, we are not limited by descriptions of other people. And we are not really defined by our own labels. These labels only refer to our mask, not to our true identity. No need to take it personally.

And there is another thing. All these definitions and descriptions are concepts, and they are all witnessed. By whom or by what are they perceived? It all happens in the spaciousness which is not different from our "I am" – the pure is-ness which we all share and are. Nondualism is not a belief system that tries to find a way to get your ego free from labelling, it rather points to the space in which those labels arise.

Q: And seeing the aware space as the unchanging witness already takes out the juice of these labels. They have less impact. There is a 'zooming out' of our camera from limitation to spaciousness. And it becomes clear that there is no need to get rid of the mask.

JK: That may be one of the secondary effects of being clear about this. But nothing can leave any footprints in aware beingness. Even an experience of deep silence and bliss will pass. The things we experience, they come and go, they are like passengers in transit. But the airport itself is not in transit.

Q: So, I should pay more attention to the witnessing than to the experience which is witnessed?

JK: The question is, who would be doing that? Who should pay more attention to anything? Remember that the 'me' is not involved in this. We must realize that all my metaphors have limited value.

Q: But the airport doesn't judge or categorize the travelers in transit. All the things which come and go are changing. So, we just stay here as the aware space?

JK: And maybe that is exactly what 'we' are all already doing anyway.

Q: Right. We - as aware beingness - are already a neutral witness. But it doesn't feel like that for my ego.

JK: If you have had a nice sensation, you probably want to push the repeat button, you probably want to play that same record again and again. But that is not the goal of these experiments and these conversations. If you have had a painful sensation, you probably want to avoid playing that 'bad record' again. You might want to push the erase button, you want to forget about the bad experiences you had. Or you try to find out how to avoid having such a painful experience again in the future. In nondualism, we do not point to the person who is struggling with all this, but we point to that which doesn't struggle. Our attention may go from here to there, even from past to future, but the impersonal awareness in which these are witnessed, doesn't go from here to there, from past to future.

Q: Where will this lead to?

JK: When you have a specific goal, you limit yourself. It is like looking for a specific tree in a dark forest with a flashlight, you only see where you are pointing your flashlight. And your attention goes from here to there as well. However, without a flash light, our eyes need to adjust to the darkness and we may feel a bit lost in the beginning. But soon our eyes get used to the darkness and we may be overwhelmed by the full picture, by the unlimited view where all options are open. We might see that between the trees in this forest, there is a vast empty space. Did we ever sense the subtlety of this space? And we are walking in the middle of that space. Between sounds, there is silence, between thoughts there is awareness. Between the mental battles in our heads there is peacefulness.

Q: And 'it' was there – or here - before it was recognized as such.

JK: And the space between the trees is made of the same basic elements as the trees itself.

When one writes
about nondualism,
one is already compromising
from the first word.
It's unavoidable.
Even trying to *point* to
the unfindable
is also an attempt
which will always fail.

Chasing Clouds

Q: I have attended an interesting group meditation. First, we were invited to leave behind our past and future. And then we just had to remain as empty presence. And then we were asked, what is left - if all concepts of the mind are thrown in the fire? What cannot be thrown away? And then, we felt an empty space which was very familiar and full and silent.

JK: The sense of 'I am' can't be thrown away. It is like an empty space. I believe that such moments of deep recognition of that space, as you describe, can be very inspiring. This space knows no disappointments, no competition, no ambition, no seven steps to heaven. It just *is*. And then we might wonder, what is the difference between what we really are and this spaciousness? How far is it away from what we are?

Q: There is no distance, which means that this space is what we really are, always have been, always will be. It was such an inspiring moment.

JK: Don't turn it into an experience you had, by saying that it was such an inspiring moment. Because then you give it to the ego. The parrots in your head come on stage and say that they own this experience. Don't believe these voices. You give it to the past, as if it disappeared after the experiment you did there. Don't fall into that trap. And you may also wonder, to whom was this experience appearing? What is aware of this recognition of this space? Did this space come from somewhere? Did you see it enter the room during the experiment? Do you believe that the space can walk away from you?

Q: In this space, there was no seeker. Just being without waiting. And no person inside. Nobody home.

JK: During such moments, it may become clear that a seeker who is trying to get in a higher state of consciousness is just chasing clouds.

Q: All you ask us is to stop chasing special states. And not to feed the spiritual ego with new rules and new goals. Do you want us to leave behind all our personal ambitions as well?

JK: I am not asking you anything, because that would only confirm your ego in its central position. I am only pointing out that you were taking your inner voices seriously. Maybe these parrots in your head are frauds, storytellers, liars. Just let life flow. This takes no effort. But the spiritual ego is never satisfied. The so-called spiritual ego is like the human ego, but its interest lies in the spiritual field. It is the sense of being a seeker. The spiritual ego is always hungry. When it is having breakfast, it thinks about lunch. When it is having lunch, it asks what's for dinner. The spiritual ego may be very clever and play the game of being an expert in nondualism, by repeating the words from the books of Advaita or Zen. It will say, I am nobody, I am only living in the timeless, there is nowhere to go - but maybe all these words are coming from the spiritual ego.

Q: These are voices in the mind. These are the parrots talking again.

JK: These voices can be so smart and eloquent that one doesn't realize it is just a parrot repeating some wise words. But it usually stays on the mental level. I call it a spiritual ego for the sake of explaining this, but in fact this spiritual ego has not a real consistency, so I already give it to much value. It is another concept after all. It is like the top of your wave, there is a white part at the crest of the wave. That is your spiritual ego. It is made of the same water as the rest of 'your' wave. But bear in mind that all my metaphors are doomed to fail, it is impossible to explain this space in words. I can only say what it is not. And even that is difficult.

Q: So that spiritual ego is something which is typically found among spiritual seekers, right? And these spiritual seekers are not so much interested in new shoes or a new apartment or a conventional family life, but they want spiritual liberation. So, they have an additional need. Or a higher goal in life than normal people.

JK: We always search for experiences, but all of it is temporary. This applies for both our human ego as well as our spiritual ego. It is endless. Why not focus on that which stays? We look for experiences, and forget the space in which the experiences come and go.

Q: But when clarity has come, will I still be able to enjoy life? Can we still enjoy going to a restaurant and drink wine with friends? Travel around the world? Can we continue to enjoy the company of our family? I love my children. I love a long table with my family for brunch on Sunday. I love to go shopping with my sisters.

JK: All these things you mention are also expressions of the same oneness, so why would you exclude anything at all? In some traditions, there have been very strict rules of conduct, but in nondualism none of that remains. Even the sense of being a man or a woman with certain needs and friends and likes and dislikes, that is all natural to a certain extent. There is no need to fight against certain needs or habits.

Q: I just give them space. I let them be.

JK: It is enough to be clear about what you really are and notice the difference with what you always believed to be. In presence of other people who are not into this, you still pretend to be a person with a future and a past, you don't talk about nondualism with them. It is better to remain silent. The role you play can just go on. You are a daughter when you visit your parents, you are a mother when you are playing with your children, you are a sister with your sisters, you are a lover when you are in bed with your husband, you are a colleague when you are at work, and so on. But behind all these roles, there is absolute clarity that you are none of these. Even when you feel bad because you had an argument with your boss, even then the spaciousness is still there. Don't listen to that parrot that says, "You see, you are not there yet, because you had a fight with your boss." Nothing can stain this spaciousness.

Q: It is like an actor playing a role. Or several roles.

JK: What we really are doesn't depend on the roles we play, and yet it is inside the core of every role we play. Being clear about this doesn't mean you must shave your head, eat only vegetables, wear orange robes and become celibate. Life can be celebrated. When we realize we are the ocean, how can we start to fight the wave on the surface? How can the deep waters be judgmental about the conduct, size and height of the waves on the surface? They are all made of the same water anyway. Don't you see that this is all extremely simple and obvious? How could clarity ever ask you to turn your back to life, to act unnaturally. In nondualism, nobody is asking you to sit alone in your chair and retire from society, unless that feels natural for you. If this would feel natural to you, you can become a Buddhist nun as well, and follow the 227 rules of conduct. There are no rules in nondualism. No obligations. How could anyone say that eating your favorite food with a glass of wine with your friends is not allowed?

Q: So, you are freed from the role you sometimes need to play, this role of being a serious spiritual seeker.

JK: There is no addiction to try to be spiritual. And there is no attachment to that pleasure of eating and drinking and loving either. And no need to criticize the priests or nuns who live a very strict life. No labeling. That which you really are doesn't have to go out and pursue pleasure outside of itself when the source of true contentment is found inside. Well, it is not inside, the separation between inside and outside is also an idea. But pleasure will come, pain will come, life takes care of all that. But the witness which sees all this remain untouched. It notices our pain and pleasure, our attachments to pleasure and our fear for pain, and 'it' doesn't need to go anywhere. So maybe one could say that a clear mind leaves more room for life as it is. It's always fresh. Life flows as it flows, just like a river.

Q: Someone who is still strongly attached to its position as a serious spiritual seeker on a specific spiritual path may feel more rigid, and act less natural. If you are very rigid about following certain rules of a spiritual organization, this may lead to a certain unnaturalness, because you are very busy in keeping up the self-image you have of yourself. You are always worried if you are not braking one of the rules of your community. You must be vigilant about the image you show to the other members of that organization.

JK: We have adopted the mask of a man or a woman, but some also wear the hat of the spiritual seeker on top of our head. And in some cases, that is an extra burden. But it is not always a burden. For some people, their spiritual role has been a tremendous gift. A lot of people find solace in a religious community. That's totally fine. They learn about compassion and helping other people in the monastery or ashram. They may experience a sense of being together for a good purpose, and that's fine as well. And if someone finds inner peace and true contentment in a temple in the mountains, that's also fine. In nondualism, spiritual or religious behavior is not criticized. It is part of the 'what is' as well.

Q: But in many cases, it is just an extra burden.

JK: It can be. We are only pointing out a mechanism of the human mind. We are not suggesting that one lifestyle is superior over the other.

Q: So according to nondualism, you start with taking off the *spiritual* hat on top of your head. And because of nondual wisdom, the mask of the *human* ego becomes more transparent.

But you said that according to nondualism, there are no rules. And there is no homework. Does this mean that anything we want to do is fine now?

JK: This mainly applies to the *religious* codes of conduct. As I said before, these spiritual rules lose their meaning. Nondual wisdom leads to the melting away of all spiritual hierarchies. The hat of the saint is blown away by the wind.

The other rules are still there, of course, and they are interesting mainly for practical reasons. The rules of society can help you to move into the world with respect to others. You stop for a red light and you drive on for a green light. You help your fellow people if you can. But that is on the human level.

On the so-called spiritual or religious level, there is no more heaven and hell, no more angels and devils, no more karma and guilt. You can still read the holy books, but you might read them now with a whole different mindset. You might see that some parts have been (re)written by people who had no clarity, and other parts are pure nondualism. You might smile while reading the first text and be surprised by the universal wisdom expressed by the second text. But once all is clear, there is no more need to even confirm this or to check this out.

Even the religious rules are fine, they are also a part of the expression of oneness. Nothing or nobody is excluded.

There's no reader,
just the cartoon strip.
There seems to be a story
of a protagonist,
but there's just
a series of images
made of black lines
on white paper.

Are We Being Lived?

Q: Some teachers of nonduality say that we are all being-lived.

JK: Whatever happens through us in each moment is a result of many natural laws. These laws make the planets orbit around the sun, make the clouds pass by, make the trees grow, make the dogs bark and make humans do what humans do. And in a way, it is true that we are the result of thousands and thousands of impulses which seem to influence our operating system. All these impulses follow the laws of nature.

Q: Some say that all events simply happen, we can't control or steer all of them at the same time because there are way too many influences. They are beyond our control. If I want to make the proper decision, I have hundreds of items I should take in consideration. And I can't do that. It's impossible to make the perfect decision.

JK: Our DNA is made of the genes of our parents and grandparents, so that is out of our control as well. And our language and habits are mainly created by our parents and the society in which we grew up. We don't control all these things completely. And we could wonder if all the thoughts, urges and emotions which arise in our body and mind, are also just appearing on their own accord. They seem to drive us to behave in a certain way, they seem to influence us in a way. But it is interesting to wonder if all this just happens on its own, automatically. Maybe everything is just happening, no matter what we feel about it or no matter how we think about it.

Q: I can understand that I don't create these stimuli, I want to accept that they just happen automatically. If the same would be true for my feelings and deeds, I could say that I am not living my life, I'm being-lived.

JK: If this would be true, your ego may feel it lacks control. But there may also be a sense of relief. So much psychological thinking falls away. So many spiritual stories about heaven and hell lose their power. When it comes to guilt and regret, you are off duty. However, this also applies to the pleasant thoughts of the mind. Your phantasies and personal pleasures are also related to your sense of being a personality. They would lose impact as well.

Q: So, it works both ways.

JK: But remember, your question regarding free choice or no free choice is still coming from the ego. This story of 'not having free will' still applies *to the person*. It may feel good for some seekers to hear that their master in Bombay said that there is no doership, that everything is just happening. You might conclude, "I am just being-lived."

If the person is taken for real, you are still giving importance to such questions. These concepts still point to the person you think you are. It may be a character without doership now, but the focus is still on the person.

Q: Doership or no doership, it is still pointing to the sense of personhood?

JK: Nondualism will mainly question the sense of personhood itself. On the other hand, if you are looking for some relief on the personal level, the belief that there is no decider and no doer is very attractive.

And don't worry that when this realisation settles in, you turn into a villain. Most people feel a sense of release and naturalness when they see that there is no doer. They find it even obvious that there is only the *idea* of a doer.

And as there is also less judging and labelling, a natural intelligence starts to take over the steering wheel.

Q: And these people say that life seems to flow more smoothly.

JK: Being clear about all this brings sometimes a sense of ordinariness, because everyday life is more than enough. No need to be in a higher state any more. Your spiritual ego is not trying to get somewhere else anymore!

And yet, there is also a magnificence about this. It is ordinary and stunning at the same time.

There's no need to
describe yourself.
It's only a mask.
There's no need to
assess your spiritual status.
It's only a hat.
Our natural beingness
doesn't need any of these two.

A Bridge Between the Wave and the Ocean

Q: Sometimes I feel very relaxed and content for no reason. There is peace inside. The sense of a person is still there but is more like somewhere in the background. My ego is hardly noticeable. Then something happens and the person rushes to the fore again, for example to judge, react, plan or regret. I will have to try to accept this oscillation between foreground and background.

JK: This apparent going back and forth could be described as the oscillation between personhood and presence. There is no going from one to the other, of course, we just use these words to make it clear. Don't conclude it is hundred percent of personhood when you are for example angry or when you are feeling down, even then presence is full on. It's simply less obvious to your mind. And don't expect it can become hundred percent of presence when you are for example in deep peace and silence, even then a minimal sense of personhood will be there. The sense of personhood might be unrecognized, but something might be still there to be able to function in society. Don't worry about that either. Maybe when you are in deep sleep, the sense of personhood is switched off completely, I don't know. But that oscillation between personhood and presence should not receive so much attention.

Q: Why not?

JK: Is that oscillation still watched with interest? If yes, then there is still a personal interest there. Are you still trying to get more presence and less personhood? The one who is checking this out is again a voice of the spiritual ego. It is another parrot coming on stage. The ultimate isn't interested in this apparent oscillation. Beingness cannot be stained if there's more personhood. It can't be bothered if the person is behaving in a certain way. What we really are is never absent. No spiritual gymnastics are needed here, no spiritual checklist, no pilgrimages or change of diet is required. And yet, all of it is 'allowed' as well.

Q: I want to know how close I am to the top of the mountain.

JK: Don't ask yourself whether you are almost there. No measurement is necessary. It's another trick of the spiritual ego to stay alive. It's not about you anyway, so why give attention to such thoughts? Don't compare yourself as a seeker now with you ten years ago. You are looking for progress or evolution. That would again be about your personality. You see, it's one of those voices again. I always say you need no effort to see this, but if you insist on trying, then I would say, just be clear about this. Notice that the spiritual ego uses several tools to stay alive, like identification, labelling, time, causality and space.

Q: But I want to get rid of the ego completely. I need to destroy it.

JK: Even when you really want to end the search, and the ego says, let's kill that ego, do you really believe that such a voice is reliable? I wouldn't trust that lady in your skull. No need to plan your own disappearance. It is like a snake which pretends to bite itself to death.

Q: The snake is only *pretending* to bite its own tale?

JK: On the other hand, this snake has no venom. It's like these cobra's in India which come out of a wicker basket when someone plays the flute. They look poisonous, but their venom glands have been removed. So, whenever I am referring to the spiritual ego, it is less venomous than we think it is.

Q: There are also many moments when I feel as if I have – finally - reached the top.

JK: The ego has many special tricks to keep itself alive. Like in a poker game, it will come up with a special card to stay in the running. In some cases, it will come up with the pride card, which says that you are better than the others. And maybe you feel better than other seekers because you meditate for a longer time, you are never angry, you can sit in lotus position for three hours, you never drink alcohol or you have written a book about nondualism. All these things are fine, but all I ask you is to see through the one who believes to be the owner of all this. When you are a spiritual seeker, along the mask of the human ego, you additionally have accepted a hat on your head. This hat says you are looking for something higher than the material world. It can be a religious hat, if you are Christian or Hindu, a spiritual hat when you meditate or do yoga, a Zen hat if you are into Zen, or even a nonduality hat if you are into Advaita. In the beginning you want a higher hat, because it is like a sign of progress and importance. Or maybe you are already quite familiar with nondualism and now you also want to get rid of that Advaita hat.

Q: Why is it so difficult? Each time I am about to end the search, something comes along, and I am thrown backwards again. It is as if I am standing on a bridge to liberation, and each time I make some progress, the bridge itself becomes longer. I believe I will never make it.

JK: Don't put your tent on that bridge. Don't get hooked on a path. Here again the spiritual ego is playing the cards which work for you, like the failure card which says that *you* are never going to get 'it.'
But all these cards only can trick you if you believe to be a person who is on a journey. It only matters if you believe to be a person who is separate from beingness, who is made of a different substance than

beingness. The wave believes to be different form the ocean, and tries to find a bridge between the wave and the ocean. Maybe your ego can be tricked but aware beingness cannot be tricked.

Q: I try not to get back into personhood.

JK: No need to get aroused by any personal game which tricks you back into identifying less with body. No need to get disappointed when you notice more identification with your self-image. It is another subtle form of labelling yourself. You are looking in the mirror and studying your mask.

Q: It is a waste of time. But there are some situations where I feel that all my experience with meditation and yoga are not strong enough to keep me centred in my true essence. Some people or some situations seem to be able to reactivate my sense of person.

JK: Each seeker has such a weak point, a field in life which easily seduces you. The parrots know that. When we are vigilant, these mechanisms may be seen through. You can still enjoy the company of your partner and your family, take care of your business, enjoy sensuality, sex and good food, enjoy the company of your friends, but these cannot take you off track.
The main dish remains the natural sense of being what we are, the white canvas which remains untouched. Nothing can attack your true being, even

not the strongest tornado of egocentric rage or deep sadness can do it. After the tornado, the space remains untouched.

The parrots in your mind
will seduce 'your' ego
with clever questions like
how, why and when.
If you go deeper into that,
they keep you busy
and then they will bite.

Lost in Thought

Q: In mindfulness meditation, we are asked to overcome our imprisonment within the confines of our own thoughts. It is said that most people are guided by their thoughts and their emotions and can't have a natural life any more. Most people – and even more so those 'normal people' who never meditate or never practice yoga - seem to have lost their original sense of pure being completely. When they would join a conversation about aware beingness, they would wonder what we are talking about. They simply have no clue. They never leave the path of conventional thinking, which is conditioned by their education and their past. And even seekers who are into yoga and meditation are still struggling with their own thoughts. How can we go beyond thought?

JK: While you ask this question, an image comes to my mind of a young girl I saw walking her dog in a local park. She is a tiny girl of say 9 years old, and received a puppy for her birthday. When the dog is still small, the girl can easily manage the little dog. But when the puppy starts to grow and becomes bigger and stronger, the girl isn't able any more to manage the dog. Now it is the dog walking the girl, instead of the other way around.

Q: She is being pulled from this side to the other side.

JK: For some people, it is the same with their thoughts. Our thoughts should be our servants, because they warn us and guide us in everyday life. And that is great. We need them for all sorts of things. We learn to read and write and all the rest. They are great tools to manage our lives in modern society. But at some point, the thoughts start living their own lives. These thoughts have no practical value, they only serve the ego and its fears and desires. Especially when we wake up at 3 am in the night, these thoughts are sometimes overwhelming, and we can't find the button to switch them off. Even during the day, we can't put them in perspective any more. So, for many people, their thoughts become their masters. The puppy has turned into a strong Doberman.

Q: Some people really seem to have several dictators in their heads. And these thoughts also bring in their friends, emotions. And even physical reactions. With some people this is obvious, because when you observe them you can see that they immediately act out their thoughts. Since I have been practicing yoga and meditation, I am more aware of my inner parrots, all these voices which take away my sense of inner peace. But I must admit that during the day, the voices and emotions come up again while I don't want them to come up. On the outside, I look very calm and friendly, but inside there is a lot of frustration and judging.

JK: You are right, even people who are practicing mindfulness or yoga may still complain that some thoughts seem to come again and again, whether they like it or not. But I don't think one needs to start a battle against these thoughts. That would be another additional source of stress. Notice that we are also *labeling* these thoughts. The thoughts appearing is one thing, our additional comments on these thoughts is a second issue. Some thoughts we like, others we don't like. We don't mind if peaceful thoughts are appearing. We don't mind if pleasant thoughts are returning in our consciousness. But we don't want thoughts which are not kind or respectful. We don't want thoughts which make us feel worried or sad. And yet, they might appear. Sometimes we are happy that other people can't read our thoughts during such a moment. They might come unexpectedly while we are sitting in a train or while we are performing a ceremony in our temple or church. And they haunt us when we wake up in the middle of the night. They show up at the party with no invitation.

Q: How do we deal with those thoughts? Should we try to be without any thoughts? Should we focus our attention more on the space between two thoughts? Should we try to find the on/off button so that we can decide when to switch our thoughts off?

JK: Trying to control our thoughts is not impossible, but it demands a lot of training and energy. Some yogi's and Zen masters are said to be without thoughts for long periods of time, but I don't think this is going to be a practical or a very interesting method for people like you and me. I am not able to stay without thoughts for a long time, but I don't consider that as an issue. There is another way to look at your question. Another approach is simply not to pay attention to these thoughts. You don't label them. You don't say to the beautiful thoughts to stay and to the ugly thoughts to go to the exit. You do not fight them, you don't try to suppress them, but you don't overrate them either. When you notice a certain thought, where does it come from? It is like the clouds in the sky. There is a blue sky, and then suddenly there is a small white cloud. And a bit later it is bigger and turns grey. Then the whole sky turns dark grey. No more sunshine. Then it rains. And one hour later the sky is blue again. Where did these clouds go to? So, trying to fight against the clouds is like fighting against the laws of nature. It is like trying to have a sky with only white clouds. Or even a blue sky with no clouds at all. It feels like struggling against the wind. I believe it is easier to just watch clouds passing by and not overrate them. And when there is a blue sky without clouds, it is a bonus.

Q: This is the easy way, you simply don't pay much attention to them. It sounds a bit too easy to me.

JK: But I don't say this to bring you into a state of serenity. This is not a technique I recommend so *you* - as a seeker - will attain a special state of peace and serenity in the future. You - as a person - don't need an upgrade. Your mask is fine as it is. I am not going to spend our time in putting the right make-up on your mask. In nondualism, we usually don't go into these questions for long, but point again and again to that spaciousness in which these thoughts come and go. Every thought – and every emotion – is temporary, it comes and goes. Even when you feel a certain emotion is there for years, say depressive feelings, they disappear each night during the dreamless sleep.

Q: They even disappear for a second when someone rings the bell or when you witness a car accident.

JK: Exactly.

Q: Nothing stays forever.

JK: Instead of focusing on the thoughts, we focus on the space in which these thoughts come and go. Although that aware space can't be seen or described, it cannot be denied either. It is aware of our thoughts, emotions and sense perceptions. It is even aware of our sense of personhood. And yet, it is not separate from all these things either. They are even made of the same ingredients. There is no separation, except in our minds.

Q: Why are these voices in my head so persistent?

JK: It is like great white sharks, they need to keep on swimming to stay alive. They ventilate their gills by swimming with their mouths open to extract oxygen from the water. If they stop swimming, they can't survive. They would run out of oxygen. It is typical for the great white shark. It is the same with the spiritual ego, it needs to keep talking itself into business or it will die. Those egocentric voices really scream for attention to stay alive, to keep up the puppet called ego. And they will do anything to make the puppet look like a real human being. These voices can seduce you, make you proud, make you anxious or make you tremble. This can happen during the day while you are sitting in your car or these voices can also wake you up in the middle of the night. All these are games in your own mind, but these voices need an audience to seduce or frighten.

Q: If there's a strong belief in the identification with my personhood, and the limits of the body are my only reality, these voices have a foot in the door. As long as there's a person who beliefs in time, they can come back.

JK: Time is a strong weapon of the ego. Memory is one of its favourite tools. Unmasking the time monster is another trick to unmask the parrots. The parrots love past and future. Time seems to eat almost everything. Every thought, every emotion, every experience you ever had, it is swallowed by the time monster. All that's left are some vague memories. But there's one thing which time can't swallow, and that's the awareness. It is like the Pacman game on the computer. The little yellow monster can eat these dots endlessly, but it can't eat the screen. So, all your concepts will be eaten by time, but 'you' as presence cannot be eaten by time. For the screen, there is no beginning nor an end to that computer game. The screen didn't mind that the dots were eaten. The screen did not give any comments. The screen will not regret when the game is over. The screen remains as it is, neutral and untouched. In nondualism, it is said that what we really are, is the borderless screen.

Q: You talked about the egocentric voices. Are there also other voices which are not egocentric?

JK: As I said before, some voices whisper that what we really are is this aware beingness. Usually these voices remain under the radar because there is so much noise from the other thoughts and perceptions. One doesn't hear the nightingale's song when there is a lot of traffic inside our head. But there may be moments of unplanned silence and timelessness, where suddenly *it* becomes clear (to no-one). Some people hear these voices during meditation or while being in nature. Other people have reported that this nightingale's song appeared unexpectedly when they were in a very threatening situation, where everything in their life seemed to be lost, when all hope was gone.

Q: Yes, I heard about stories of prisoners who found liberation in the concentration camps, or criminals who discovered absolute freedom the day before they were put on the electric chair.

JK: Yes. It is an illustration of the black leading to the white. When all is lost, when there is no hope, the parrots might be completely silent because there is no future anyhow. And then, the other voices may whisper in your ear, so to speak.

Q: These voices are pointing to the aware space that we really are. They point to our source of peace inside.

JK: Exactly. They remind us of the love and silence *within*, which is also *without*.

No need to embark
on a great search
in order to become
aware of awareness.
Who would do it?
Who would attain what?
This spaciousness is
completely unfindable
and yet it's never absent.

Die Before You Die

Q: As human beings, we all must live with one inescapable certainty, the idea that we are lined up in death row awaiting our execution.

JK: If 'you' feel identified with 'your' body, and if you believe your ego is moving from the past to the future, then the question is not whether you will die, but only *when* you will die. You feel you are sitting on a ship that is surely going to sink. But that is a very materialistic view. It's a very limited vision.

Q: However inevitable the end of the body-mind may look, the crucial question is if death is really the end. Is there a helicopter on my boat, so I can fly to heaven when the ship is sinking?

JK: Are you an actor on a screen or are you the light in the images? Person or presence? Wave or ocean? In other words, are you asking this question from a human perspective or a being perspective?

Q: I believe I am a person. And I realize that my fear for death is related directly to my ego.

JK: Everybody has the sense of being a person in a body occasionally, so do I. It's fine. That is how we are brought up. And you better have a minimum sense of personhood when it is necessary, otherwise you will end up in a mental hospital. This ego inside of us is part of our human conditioning. It is the wave that comes up and disappears after say 80 years of life on this planet. We are conditioned to limit ourselves to this wave. And that is also fine to a certain extent. But there is more. Because despite this worldwide conditioning of identifying with a limited identity, one may also recognize the being part in each of us. And it is not a separate part in us which is separate from the others, it is the one beingness with no limits.

Q: So, it is ok that my mind and senses say that I am in this body.

JK: Yes, that is how they are designed. When you are standing in a crowded train of the subway and someone steps on your right toe, you might say that there is nobody inside your body, but still the pain appears in your right toe and not in your left toe. And the pain doesn't appear in the toe of the person standing next to you. It is how our nervous system works.

Q: No need to deny that.

JK: But when we talk about nondualism, we are not only pointing at the physical level, not only at the human level. If you believe that you are made of perishable stuff, death simply means that the game is over. Once the heart stops beating, the brain will run out of oxygen and soon after that, the movie is over.

Q: The ship sinks. Over and out. But I sense that this can't be true. I say to myself, my body may be made of perishable stuff, but what about my soul? My personality does not want to disappear, and therefore I like to believe in a life after my physical death. The captain will leave his ship behind and fly to heaven. That's maybe why I like the existence of a soul. *My* soul. It's attractive because then my story isn't over when I die. It prevents me from vanishing into nothing, into a black hole or something. And such a story about a soul leads to fascinating stories about an afterlife or reincarnation.

JK: Such stories have always been popular. From the Egyptians to the Buddhists and Hindus, there are plenty stories around. But as you say, it is still about *your* soul, it is still about you. Nondualism points to that which *everybody* is.

Q: All these religions seem to have some sort of story about what happens after you die. Doesn't that illustrate that there must be an afterlife after death?

JK: The number of people who believe in a story is not relevant when checking if something is true or not true.

Q: But deep down I believe I am still afraid of dying.

JK: That's a completely different issue. That makes you vulnerable. And to deal with that fear you are willing to accept stories which can't be verified. Some people are excellent in spotting your weak points and in taking advantage of them. They will give you a story of heaven and hell. You accept their stories because they make you feel better. Or because you feel accepted in a large group of people who believe in the same story. When you are not clear about what you really are, you are likely to cover your fear or uncertainty by such games of the mind. If you are certain about something, you don't need to believe in anything. Then you don't care about heaven and hell. But you don't tell these people that you are right and that they are wrong, that would be another form of dualism. You just keep quiet.

Q: It sounds as if you know what happens when you will die.

JK: No, of course not. That's impossible.

Q: And what about the stories about heaven and hell? Or about reincarnation? They exist for more than 3000 years.

JK: They're still stories. All these stories are not attractive any more as soon as there is clarity about our true nature. When it's clear that time and personhood are concepts, all these stories lose their significance immediately.

Q: You also said that they don't mean much because they are not absolute.

JK: Because they are different in each tradition. For example, Christianity sees these items completely different than Hinduism. Still both claim to know the absolute truth. Each religion comes with a different story. The ancient Egyptian book of dead tells a different story than the Tibetan book of dead. The idea about heaven and hell is also different for Islam and Judaism.

Q: If they all come with a different story, you tend not to believe any of them.

JK: That's it. Their value is local, not global. Nondualism looks for a theory that is true for everyone, not for one group of people.

Q: So, nobody knows how it feels to be dead.

JK: But on the other hand, it may be possible that the pure beingness which we *are* right now is the same as the beingness that 'awaits us' when we die. Well, it isn't really waiting for us, of course. That's just a way to explain things. All I want to say is that what you really are – boundless energy – is not affected by death. Your body is born and will die, but beingness is out of time. Birth and death are each other's opposite, but life is eternal. Well, not eternal in the usual sense that it goes on forever, it is *timeless*. The aware beingness does not play the game of coming and going. It doesn't know what time is. It just is.

Q: When we die, the film runs out, but the white screen is still there. The light in the back of the theatre is still on. That's the point you want to make, isn't it?

JK: Beingness doesn't stop when the film stops because is-ness has no limits in time and space.

Q: It is immortal, it is endless.

JK: When both the ego and time are purely conceptual, then both birth and death must be conceptual too. It is like water recognizing its wetness. When the concept of 'me' melts away, death is like an ice cube of water melting away in a glass of water. Death is also a reminder to the impermanent nature of all life forms. Death is at the same time an invitation to discover that timelessness within us which doesn't die.

Q: I remember one day you used the metaphor of the sandcastles. We are all made of molecules which are made of atoms. These atoms are made of protons and electrons. So, one could say that on the atomic level we're all built of the same basic elements.

JK: We're all made of sand grains.

Q: So, all human beings are like sandcastles who believe that they're separate from the other sandcastles because they all have a different shape. And from my personal point of view, I seem to have an individual shape. Different from yours, for example.

JK: Right. In the daytime dream, each one of us has a unique genetic code, and a unique body with a unique shape. And our senses confirm each day that we seem to be separate. Each wave seems to have its own particular story.

Q: Exactly. That's what I find so difficult. My five senses tell me I am separate and then I read in your book we are all one. I don't feel that way. It feels to me that each one of us is a separate person.

JK: I know. It is the same here. There is a sense of a person called Jan residing in this body. That's how the brain works. That's how the senses and memory and all our conditionings work together. My parents have put a flag on top of my sandcastle with the name Jan, but that is also another concept.

Q: To me, however, it's clear that each one of us is living in his or her private sandcastle. That's how it appears to me!

JK: What you say is true. It *feels* that way. It's even meant to feel that way. Otherwise we wouldn't take the movie for real. Maybe life is just designed that way.

Q: We are supposed to feel separate.

JK: We are not supposed to feel separate or united or anything else. Whatever you believe you feel like, it's still an idea. And that idea is another snapshot on the screen.

Q: You mean that the sense of separation is itself also an idea. Just another image? And the same for the sense of oneness.

JK: Right.

Q: I see.

JK: What if the water in the ice cube understands it is water? What if the light sees that basically all actors *are* the same single light? One endless desert of sand with 8 billion sandcastles. As soon as we see that we are sand rather than a sandcastle, it becomes clear that all separation is in our minds. It is all purely conceptual. And as a result, identification with the body is conceptual too. What we essentially are – aware beingness – has no limits and can't die. But thinking about the infinite is not the same as the infinite.

Q: So, I am immortal?

JK: No, it's not about *you*. What you believe you are is an image and that's even not capable of living for more than a few seconds. But what you really are is timeless and cannot die.

Q: Can you prove this theory to me? Are you speaking from your own experience?

JK: No, of course not. Infinity can't be experienced. The person can't attain immortality. It's aware beingness which is immortal. Because it is *before* time. It's timeless.

Q: But when my character dies, it won't be acting any more. My movie will be over!

JK: As soon as the sandcastle is destroyed, it disappears into the rest of the desert. The sand grains might be recycled or redistributed in a random way, I don't know, but its unique shape is gone. From dust to dust, from sand to sand. The game is over.

Q: That's what I am saying. Game over!

JK: But at the same time, 'your' true essence – being sand – can't disappear.

Q: In your metaphor, the sand grains have survived physical death. The children have destroyed their castle at the end of the day, but the sand grains can't be destroyed.

JK: What happens is that the body-mind machine dissolves into the ocean of beingness, just like a wave that disappears in the ocean. Just like an ice cube melting away in a glass of water.

Q: You go back to the light.

JK: No, it's not 'you' going back to the light or to heaven or whatever. The real you – pure beingness - is already all and everywhere. So, 'it' doesn't have to go somewhere when the body dies.

Q: So, it's just an image on the screen that won't come up any more. I wonder how life will be without me. I mean, does everything just go on, without me? And without my soul going somewhere else? I find that hard to accept. It doesn't sound attractive to me.

JK: Others say that really seeing this or clearly understanding this, gives them a sense of relief. They now look at physical death as complete liberation.

Q: What is the difference between death and liberation?

JK: I don't know what liberation really means. But if there is a clarity about what we are, and we see the difference between what we really are and what we *think* we are, the story of life may be seen as a conceptual story. If this happens before your body dies, there is liberation from the personal. There is clarity while the movie still goes on. When you die, it is probably the same, but then the movie stops as well. In both cases, the person is absent.

When the wave
falls back into the ocean,
can it report about
its own disappearance?

Stuck in the Seeking Process

Q: I feel like I am stuck in this seeking process. I am following your pointings for a long time, and I do have moments of peace and serenity. But then suddenly, I feel stuck again.

JK: I don't deny that you may experience a sense of stuckness. It is very common. But let's take some time to examine what exactly is going on. We start to look at your question by checking out that sense of stuckness. I am not saying it is not real. If stuckness showed up, it was there. And it felt real to you. It was a feeling, a thought or some personal conclusion. Sometimes it may be accompanied by physical sensations and emotions of being incapable of doing this search properly. Or you complain that the seeking is taking so long. You may even have a sense of being a failure on the spiritual level, that you failed personally.

Q: Yes, I have had such moments as well. Then I think to myself, how long is it still going to take me?

JK: But how much meaning do these thoughts and feelings really have? First, they are temporary. They are not there 24 hours a day, seven days a week, are they? And when they are in the picture for a few moments, are they really referring to you as you really are or are they labels on your self-image? Don't they describe rather the idea you have about who you are? Aren't these labels you put on your mask? It is important to make the difference, so we can identify the one who is stuck. The person can believe to have a sense of being stuck, the spaciousness can't be stuck because it has no borders. As a body, as a person, as a form, you are vulnerable, but as space, as formlessness, nothing can touch you, nothing can stain you. As a person, all sorts of things may seem to happen to you, and that is inevitable. But as the space, there is no possibility of being stuck or stained.

Q: Ok.

JK: And the person who feels stuck is also being perceived. In other words, on the screen you have both an image of stuckness and an image of you. Both are seen. What perceives both this sense of stuckness and your sense of personhood?

Q: I know it is all perceived by awareness. I read it in the Advaita books. I already know this, because I have done this experiment before. I know it can be seen by awareness, but still I feel frustration.

JK: Knowing the answer doesn't count. Your answer came from memory. I am not satisfied with an answer which comes from the thinking mind. It is not fresh. I don't want to eat a salmon which is one week old. I even don't want a salmon which comes out of the fridge. It must be like a bear which catches the salmon while standing in the river. The salmon is still struggling in his mouth. That is freshness. That is how you have to respond to my answer, completely fresh. Don't get tricked by your memory.

Q: No need to run into my past. I need to stay in the moment.

JK: No. No need to say that either. Just be, without interference of the old programs. It is not enough to repeat what you have read in the books about nonduality. Then it is all mental.

Q: Then it's only in the head, not in the heart.

JK: Whether you know the answer or not, those thoughts are also perceived. No need to get caught again and again in your self-image. Your spiritual ego tries to survive in a sophisticated way, for example by *pretending* to be the witness. But that trick can also be seen by the final witness. The mask pretends to be the witness, but even then, another subtler witness is standing 'behind' that mask. It's as simple as that.

Q: Ok. But it can be frustrating sometimes.

JK: That sense of frustration is also witnessed. But the witness of the witnessing can't be witnessed.

You can only *be* that. But not you as the person, it can only be noticed by naked awareness.

Q: I think that I can't follow because my head is so full of thoughts and beliefs.

JK: In the ideal situation, we would start from zero, like a newborn. Maybe your computer is running slow because your hard disk is full and there are too many viruses in your system. But to get in that naked state of not thinking and not knowing, we should take away all your concepts and beliefs. But it is very difficult to let it all go while we are sitting here talking. Who can do that? Can you clean up your hard disk? Can you leave behind your past, your name, your qualities, your social position, your degrees? Can you forget completely about your hope for spiritual liberation? Can you clean up all the apps on your tablet or smartphone? And is it even necessary to clean it all up? And who would be doing that? Would the latter also not be another app? The cleaning app?

Q: It's way too difficult for me. These programs are rooted way too deeply in my computer. Maybe I can try to forget for two minutes my desire for liberation? Maybe I can let go all my spiritual expectations? All my religious programs? I believe I can try that.

JK: It would make things a bit easier for you if you leave your notions of heaven and hell behind. If you are a Christian, leave your Christian knowledge behind you, if you are a Hindu, leave all the religious rules behind you. Only for a few minutes. Maybe this gives you more space. But if you can't do that either, it is not a big issue. No need to make a battle of this.

Q: Ok.

JK: Simply notice that all these personal concepts were added or learned afterwards. They were not there when you were born as naked awareness. These are not your main dish. So, give these programs the position they deserve, which is the position of being side dishes. Some grilled vegetables or some Belgian fries you ordered along with the main dish.

Q: I need to look at the main dish, at what we really are.

JK: The main dish is what you were originally, even at three weeks old. And it is a white empty plate.

Q: How can I notice that? You will probably say that I – as a seeker - can't do it. But that doesn't help me.

JK: Just look without using your imagination. I also expect no labelling from you, no conceptualization.

Simply look as a baby. And then there is just this, plain is-ness. Simply the 'what is.' And then we could wonder, why not just stay with this is-ness? The senses are still functioning, you know we are sitting in a room, sitting on a chair, there may be a sense of personhood as well, but all these are not what we are. Maybe there is a desire to retain our dear personhood, and as a result the fear to lose personhood appears. It is normal that we are anxious to lose our position in society. It is normal that we are afraid to lose our position on the spiritual journey. The parrots start talking. That is where you are different from a baby. Young babies probably don't have any parrots inside their little heads.

Q: So even when I feel anxious to lose my personal identity, I don't need to fight that fear.

JK: Even this fear can be witnessed by that same aware space which witnesses all these other sensations - and which also witnesses the sense of being a person in a body. When the sense of personhood would disappear completely for one minute, what would still be here? Is there something which would still be there? If the sense of individuality disappears, the impersonal awareness hasn't disappeared. Even if you would feel like you are in free fall, even that sense is witnessed by awareness. Even if you feel extreme peace, that is also witnessed by awareness. Even if you feel deep contentment without a cause, that is also witnessed by awareness. That's why some people say that nothing can exist if it is not witnessed. We are the aware space in which all the witnessing is happening.

Q: Do I have to repeat this experiment as often as possible, until it becomes natural?

JK: No, don't turn this into a practice. Your spiritual ego wants to be back on a path. This seeing is immediate.
These experiments are a bit like looking in a mirror, where we see the reflection of our face at half a meter away from our body, and we wonder the following: are we that reflection in the mirror or are we the one who is looking from behind the eyes on 'this' side? The reflection doesn't take three seconds to appear, it is immediate.

Q: In front of the mirror my appearance – my wave – and on this side my awareness – my wetness, my ocean-ness.

JK: And no need to call it 'me' or 'mine.' That's just an old habit. The ocean and wave are not separate.

Q: It is a vast emptiness which is filled with a face on the glass of the mirror in the bathroom.

JK: Even the concept of emptiness can be a trap. Even the sense of spaciousness is only a sense. But in this space, there is no story, there are no problems, no emotions, no personal qualities, just a sense of *I am*. I can't say that you must remain as this awareness, that you *must stay* as beingness, because this can't be done by the seeker. And it can't be undone either. You can't make any mistakes. The ocean can never turn its back to a wave, how ridiculous would that be? There is only one without a second.

But the ocean itself can't be seen, oneness can't be perceived. Sometimes words are embarrassing because what I am talking about is so obvious, and every word I say is a limitation.

And I don't want to hide behind exotic terminology from the East or from any old holy books, no matter how sophisticated they are. Yet, it is completely fine to be inspired by wise words from men and women from ancient times.

Q: I read a book by Nisargadatta, its title is "I am That." It's a classic in the field of Advaita. But I find it difficult to honestly say, "I am That". I don't feel that way. Is something missing?

JK: Of course, you can't say that. A person can never honestly say, "I am That". You might say, we are That, where the word 'we' refers to the 8 billion human beings on the planet.

But even that is not true. Only the aware beingness would be able to sincerely say, "I am That". But the aware beingness has no mouth, has no sense of what awareness or endlessness is, it is mute. It would never say, "I am That". That is the moment to realize that silence is better than words.

Life flows.
Naturally.
Effortlessly.
We are that.

Not a Teaching

Q: They say that a true spiritual teacher of Advaita doesn't have anything to give or add, such as new information, new rules of conduct or new belief systems. Still there are many nondual teachers around who write books or organize dialogues about this subject. Their approach is much more modern and direct than the old teachings. I love this new wave of Advaita teachers. Can a modern teacher help us to remove that which separates us from the truth of who we really are?

JK: Yes and no. In nondualism, we are not presenting any teaching in the conventional sense of the word. When people come to a dialogue about nondualism, we address them both as separate identities as well as expressions of beingness. We address them as persons when they come into the room and pay the entrance fee at the door. We start to talk to them as if they are separate human forms, because the body and mind are our primal tools of communication during such dialogues. We pretend to be persons, like everybody else. But what the words are pointing at is that which is beyond or behind the sense of personhood.

Q: You try to point to that which is beyond the person. You need to use concepts to go *beyond* the conceptual.

JK: We cannot describe directly what aware beingness is, so we will always fail. But we can put light on the ideas and concepts in our minds which seem to veil that dimension of inner depth. And this 'deeper' dimension is stillness, peace and boundlessness.

Q: But you can't point to the boundlessness directly?

JK: Exactly. My words are no more than signposts. But don't study the signposts. We can try to point to that which is – apparently - *hiding* boundlessness. The underlying spaciousness is not created during these conversations, it was already there before our meeting started. But it might become less hidden in a way when some concepts are put in the fire. This reminds me of the Haiku written by a 17th century Japanese poet and samurai, "Barn's burnt down — now I can see the moon." If the concepts and expectations of the ego are melting away, the full moon is visible again. I would not say, "I can see the moon" but rather, "The moon is seen." Because when the roof of the thinking mind has melted away, the seeing is impersonal.

Q: There is just seeing. Not a person who is seeing.

JK: Exactly. And the moon was already there before the roof of the barn burned away. In other words, there is no need to create a moon light, it was already there anyway. In my own words, I would describe his words as follows, "When the concepts about 'my' identity melt away, the mask becomes transparent and the spaciousness is visible again." But the light was also inside the house before the roof burned away, but it wasn't recognized as such.

Q: These dialogues only unveil that which was already there. It is like cleaning the mirror which is covered by dust. Before the cleaning of the mirror, the reflection was already there but not seen clearly by the seeker. After the cleaning, the reflection reappears spontaneously. But again, I realize that this cleaning sounds like a process in time. And I know you don't like that.

JK: Exactly. No 'before and after' on the being level, but there is a *sense* of before and after on the human level. But even 'after' the clarity, we can't describe what we are, it remains impossible. It remains unattainable. We can only point to what we are not. We may use words like infinite spaciousness and aware beingness, but if these pointings are not 'followed,' these words are only meaningless concepts.

Q: Saying that there is no past and future, that there is no personhood, it is undeniably true if you are familiar with Advaita, but it may also become like cold knowledge. Especially if it is only an intellectual understanding. I have been listening to a few YouTube videos of teachers who repeat all the time that everything is nothing, that there is nobody home, and that everything is just happening. But with some of them, I got bored after a few minutes. It felt that they were repeating an idea. It felt cold, not lived. More mental than heart-felt.

JK: It is hard to tell if these teachers are talking from being or from knowing. But let's not focus on that issue. Just see for yourself. Don't worry about the so-called others. These are side dishes. I prefer to point to the empty white plate of the main dish. That is why it is interesting to follow the pointings. Don't examine the finger pointing at the moon.

Q: So, what can we do during these meetings? Just take off my grey glasses which color my perceptions, so I can see clearly again? Just go back to my original awareness as a baby? Try and clean my mirror? Clean up my computer?

JK: We try to unmask the old concepts and beliefs which seem to cover up spaciousness. It is like cleaning a mirror which is full of moisture because of high humidity in the bathroom after taking a shower. You keep wiping the moisture until you see your own reflection.

Q: When your face appears, you realize that the face was already there before the cleaning.

JK: Yes. And when you see your face in the mirror again, you may also realize that you are still looking at your mask. So, you can also wonder where you are looking *out of.* The focus is not on improving your reflection but on seeing where the witnessing takes place.

Q: Ok.

JK: One could say that what we really are is what is left when all the condensation is removed, but the latter is not correct either because the aware space is also in the moister. It was only a metaphor. Even when the mirror is full of moisture, the impersonal witness is still there. Ultimately, there is no task, there is nowhere to go, and nothing to say. In that sense, the teachers of so-called cold Advaita are right. There is no-one. No need to add a 'me' to life because life is happening anyway.

Q: I see.

JK: When people come to this kind of meetings looking for coaching, emotional healing, interesting ideas, hopeful messages or intellectual discussions, they will be disappointed. Nondualism doesn't offer much food for thought, although many concepts which we share in these conversations can be sources of deep reflection. But the insight comes rather through silence than through intellectual discussion. In the end, the essence of nondualism is not in my words but within yourself. That to which my words point is not to be found in the realm of thoughts, emotions or physical experiences. It points to the dimension which is underneath the wave, but isn't separate from the wave. The deeper layers of the ocean do not know about time or personhood, there is just space and silence.

Q: But we need to change our perspective.

JK: Rediscovering this space is like looking down through a pair of goggles while swimming at the surface of the sea. While you look down and have your ears under the water, it may become clear that the deeper layers of the ocean are without any sounds or waves. Although you are not diving like a scuba diver, but staying at the surface, this introspection may come with a deep sense of peace. But this peace is not created by your act of looking at it, it was already there. So, whenever you feel inner peace or a contentment without a cause while attending dialogues about nondualism, you know that the words are reminding you of what you really are. It is a kind of resonance. The words do not have this power of themselves, they are rather like catalysts who make this recognition possible. The signposts are not about me or about you, they are about all of us. So, they don't say, "Look at Jan," but "Look beyond both of us."

Q: And this inner stillness is what we are. And when we lose touch with that inner spaciousness, we seem to lose touch with the natural flow life.

JK: Exactly. This inner space which is beyond our usual sense of self – while it is not separate from it – is also known as the *I am*. As I pointed out before, I prefer to describe it as that what *we* are, because it points to all of us. It is the aware space in which everything is perceived. We are that awareness. We are that ocean, disguised as one wave.

In the 'what is'
there's no inside or outside,
no beginning and no end.

And Then My Ego Came Back

Q: I had a special experience a few months ago. I was meditating and then I felt melting away into everything. For the very first time, I really understood everything you said in your books. It was great. It lasted several hours. What does it mean? Was this a glimpse of liberation?

JK: Such an experience can open your eyes, it can clean your sunglasses. It is sometimes described as awareness seeing awareness. The curtains of your windows are opened, and all the light comes in. Suddenly, all the ideas you read about this subject become alive and experiential.

Q: Those who had an experience of pure light usually associate such an event with a major step on their spiritual path.

JK: Maybe that's why you asked me the question in the first place. Maybe you hoped I would say that *you* are coming closer to the end of your spiritual search because *you* had such a great transcendental event.

Q: Well, yes.

JK: If I would go into that, I would be talking to you *as a person*. But nondualism points to the *being* part of a human being, not the human part. When it's clear that the person is an idea, we can still pretend to be a person in everyday life, but we know without any doubt that the true essence is impersonal. So, you know deep inside that the person is a concept, but you don't talk about it with anyone. You just *pretend* to be a person, like everybody else. Don't forget that the so-called others are also pretending to be a real person – whether they are aware of it or not.

Q: What troubles me is that my ego came back after my awakening event. I was in a state of peace and contentment, and then my mind came back. Time also came back. I feel like I am back on the hamster wheel and searching again for liberation. Even judging appeared again. And the sense of peace was gone. What happened?

JK: What you described is quite common. There can be an unequivocal 'sensing' of just naked awareness - without anyone 'doing' it. You experienced a spontaneous moment of stillness. We could compare it with a landscape without any wind. The mind was in a state of stand-by, with no major activities.

Q: It is a relief.

JK: Yes. It is like working in a bar or a shop where there is loud music all the time. When you take your bike at the end of the day, you feel so relaxed because of the absence of noise.

Q: Nothing is added. Something disturbing just fell away.

JK: Most people experience a continuous stream of thoughts and emotions, so they are used to experience turmoil in their mind on an everyday basis. Sometimes you can tell by their body language – especially the facial expression – what they are thinking about or how they are stuck in their internal chatter. They even don't notice it and presume it is a normal thing. But in fact, it is a sort of madness, but doctors don't diagnose it as a mental disease because everybody seems to have that parasite in their heads – including the doctors themselves.

Q: Psychiatric patients sometimes hear voices, and they are diagnosed as schizophrenic because of that. Usually these voices are not very realistic, of course. They think they are the new Messiah, or they see things most people don't see like extra-terrestrials. And these alien voices ask those patients to do crazy things. But in fact, everybody is hearing voices then?

JK: We all do more or less, I guess. Some have less disturbing thoughts and emotions when they do yoga or when they practice mindfulness. Others try to escape from the turmoil of everyday life by running a marathon, going to the movies, playing a computer game, drinking alcohol or taking certain substances. In many cases their minds never stop, except of course during deep sleep.

Q: Exactly. In my daily life, I experience a stream of thoughts and emotions, but trying to stop them is not an easy task.

JK: There are several techniques to stop thoughts for a while. You can sit in lotus position and learn to stop all thinking with special breathing exercises, but sooner or later you will have to step in daily life again. At some point, a thought might appear which tells you that you are thirsty and need to drink some water, or you simply need to go to the toilet. It's pointless. But instead of trying to stop your thoughts, you can also let them pass by without paying too much attention to them.

Q: How do you mean?

JK: Imagine you are in the London subway, and the trains are passing by every few minutes. You stand in front of the train; the train opens its doors. Other passengers step in the train but you don't get in. You simply ignore the train. And then the doors close and the train takes off again. A few minutes later the next train arrives, and you do the same thing. That's a good analogy to explain what I mean. It is not something you do, it is something you don't do.

Q: You don't teach me a new technique, you simply ask me to stop repeating my old habits. So, I just stand there, and watch thoughts pass by. It sounds easier than trying to stop them.

JK: Don't try to stop the trains passing by, it's too difficult. It is like trying to stop the wind. Or trying to stop the clouds passing by. Let the thoughts and feelings come and go, just simply witness them.

Q: Most people are not capable of doing so for a long time.

JK: Maybe the voices in your head are activated again after a while, but they don't deserve all your attention. These are only some voices in your head, saying that you had 'it' while feeling peaceful and you lost 'it' while feeling normal or miserable. The reason for this is mainly a lack of clarity.

Q: How do you mean?

JK: What I am pointing at in my books is the being part of the human being. It is not a part of course, it is rather the bigger space in which the sense of being an ego could be described as a smaller space. The smaller space is the territory of the ego. It is usually described as the body and mind. In my metaphor, it is a small room within a big room. Don't take my words literally because this big room has no floor, no ceiling and no four walls because it is infinite in all directions. Anyway, we are told that we are limited to this small territory, this tiny space, this little room which is limited by the borders of our body.

Q: I see. And it feels restricted, contracted, to be locked up in this imaginary room.

JK: Right. When you have a major transcendental event, it feels like the line between your little room and the big room is melting away. The four walls, the floor and the ceiling turn from brick walls into transparent glass. That is why it can feel so spacious. The borders are gone. Sometimes, the walls of glass disappear as well. And you don't have to make any personal effort for this.

Q: Yes, it came out of the blue.

JK: And as the complaining mind is also silent at that moment, there is a sense of peace. But the silence or spaciousness was already there before the event, it was just not recognized as such.

Q: It felt so nice!

JK: Some describe it as unconditional love because the judging mind is silent, and everything is seen for what it is, without the need to change anything. But it can't be compared with romantic love or the love for your parents or for your children because in this love there is no lover and no loved one.

Q: Yes, a sense of peace, contentment and love was there. But it was not love for someone or something, it was just impersonal love. As far as I can still remember that. Words fail to describe this.

JK: When you look carefully, you may also see that at that moment, there was no person. Although this sounds like a paradox, the one who had this special experience was not home during the event.

Q: I felt like going from contraction to boundlessness. And when it was over, I was in contraction again.

JK: But the latter is also a sense, which is witnessed by the same awareness. The sense of contraction is also appearing in that bigger room, in that naked beingness. The bigger room is still there when the voices of the mind appeared again. And it is still right here right now, but you may not notice it because the curtains seem to be closed again. Don't forget that what I am trying to point at a space which is never absent.

Q: When we complain that after the sense of naked awareness, the peacefulness disappeared, we usually conclude that the ego came back. But you say that this is only the mind speaking to us.

JK: But the ego can't come back and then stay. The ego is not a solid object or a real person but only a concept of the mind, activated by decades of conditioning. The ego can't appear and disappear. The ego has no legs, it can't walk in and out. A black cat can walk on stage and walk off again during the opera, but the ego can't. What reappears is only a voice. The question is, did the stage come and go? Did the *awareness* go away when the ego appeared again?

Q: No. But why did it feel that way? Did the voices of my ego make so much noise that the original awareness was overlooked?

JK: If we are clear that the spaciousness doesn't come and go, we know that an ego thought doesn't have the power to chase the infinite away. A parrot can't chase away the room. The infinite is still there when the sense of peace and love are gone.

Q: So, what is happening then?

JK: It's like the voices of the ego come into the picture as text balloons in a comic. You sometimes see such drawings in comic books, where the character is so angry that the author illustrates this by drawing huge letters in a big text balloon.

Q: In such a drawing, almost the whole scene is covered by the words or thoughts of the main character. The text balloons are so huge that these are the only things we notice.

JK: Yes.

Q: And the white page on which the cartoon is drawn is still there, no matter what happens.

JK: Exactly. And we are also tricked by the mind in another way: through our memory. Our memory is a certified liar, it says that the ego came back to stay, but it's simply not true! The idea of being identified with the ego just popped up for a very short time. Sometimes it is a thought of a tenth of a second only. It didn't stay! Memory is a machine which is producing lies all the time. The ego did not come back, but if you believe it, you think it is true.

Q: I see.

JK: And there is another way to approach this issue. When seekers complain that after a moment of pure awareness, their ego came back, they can check if there was an ego *before* the experience of egolessness in the first place.

Q: It seemed like egolessness created timelessness. The Buddhists describe this egolessness with the term 'anatta.' There is no me. And yes, if the ego is a concept, then the disappearance must also be a concept. I never thought of that before. It's so easy. Yet, it felt lovely when time stood still.

JK: One of the things people report is indeed as if time stood still. And some people also report a state of spaciousness. And they usually say that it felt so natural and effortless. Maybe that is our original nature, who knows? Probably this is the awareness we 'had' when we were born. Before we were programmed. But don't believe now that you need to 'get' this again by practicing thoughtlessness, by 'being more present' or by 'increasing your level of awareness' or by 'trying to be more silent.' These would be new goals of the spiritual ego who believes that the 'what is' needs to be improved.

Q: Why was this seeing so spectacular the first time? A lot of seekers complain that the glimpses become less spectacular over time.

JK: When you have been locked up in a dark cellar for a long time, and you strike a match, the light is very impressive. That is the experience of bliss. But when you strike a second match five minutes later, you will be less surprised, although it is the same light. And when you put on a candle in the cellar you strike a third match, you will not be impressed any more. Even when the light is now continuous.

Q: It reminds me of that quote you posted on Facebook. You wrote: "In the middle of the night, the white light of a full moon can be quite impressive. But during the day, it's hardly recognizable."

Everything
is just happening.
Impersonally.

Speak Only if It Improves Upon the Silence

Q: I have seen a few Neo-Advaita teachers who say there's no me. They confirm from experience that the person has collapsed at some point during their spiritual search. I find that very fascinating, and I must say that the way they communicate this wisdom is intriguing. They say that the person is not real. That there is no personhood. It is a ghost. We are all ghosts, believing we are a person in a body. We are not subject to time, causality and evolution. There is just emptiness which looks like fullness. They write in their books that it is all a daytime dream. And as a result, the spiritual search is also a daytime dream. It is useless to meditate or practice spiritual techniques because there is nobody who can do it or no person to attain anything. Who would meditate? And for what goal? It's all a phantasy of the spiritual ego. And I agree upon this part.

JK: Ok.

Q: But they also say that their everyday ego – the sense of me during 'normal' life - is not real either. I find that part much harder to believe. They say that the normal ego is also a phantom. I am wondering, if the person is unreal, how can they go about in life? And why would they talk about the disappearance of their ego? I mean, if it wasn't real anyway, what is the point? What are they trying to convey? It would be like someone says, "I used to believe I am a ghost but at some point, the sense of being a ghost fell away and now I am going around to tell people they are ghosts as well." If they are ghosts as well, why would you bother telling them? Who is the knower of the belief or concept that I am a nobody? Even when they say there's nobody, that everything is nothing, that everything is just happening, who is saying that? I see words coming out of their mouth.

JK: First, let's not focus our attention on the others. That kind of conversations leads to endless discussions which are not very interesting. And one never knows if these teachers are talking from experience or from hearsay. It is hard to check if they are simply believing their own concepts. It is hard to find out if they are only avoiding the real issue by bypassing the whole game. What if we would not argue about that? Why not focus on the 'I am' and just see without comparing. Why don't we wonder what is witnessing all this? What is aware of all these words? What is aware of the sense of nobody home? What is aware of the comments on those teachers?

Q: But when I call their first name to ask a question about Advaita, they turn their heads towards me immediately. That is for me a prove that there is a sense of individuality inside them. They might deny that, and repeat that nobody is living inside their body, but I believe they are just believing their own delusions. The point is, I am in this sort of clarity for several years, but I always kept it for myself because I don't feel like talking in public about myself - or about the absence of myself. I read a book called 'Being Already Awake' or something like that, and that book was so clear and so obvious that I felt the resonance with the book and the writer immediately. And the sense of spaciousness was 'here' in a sort of impersonal way. But I must say it wasn't a personal experience in the traditional sense.

JK: I see.

Q: So, I believe I know from experience where this 'being nobody' is coming from. But still I sensed that this might become another belief. Even after experiencing it, the mind may be so clever that it even takes over this very subtle belief. So, I was at some point saying - to myself - that there is indeed nobody home. And it felt great. And I was happy to attend retreats and meet other people who seemed to have experienced the same absence of personhood. I also communicated on Facebook with other people with similar ideas.

JK: I would say, believing you are a person or believing you are not a person are both ideas in the mind. They are both clouds passing by. But the aware space remains what it is. And if the person is only a concept which we adapted from our parents, why would we bother to even mention it at all? It is only a little flag on top of our sand castle. And the flag is not even there all the time! Why give it so much attention anyway? Whether it exists or not, is not important. It surely exists as a concept, as an idea. But if some people have unmasked that entity, does it really make any difference? And to whom would it make a difference?

Q: Other teachers say that when we live without expectations, without a sense of personal choice or doership, that life will be more fluent. That we will feel deep contentment and peace. But that sounds a bit like a teaser to me. I noticed that the seekers in their audience were mainly interested in getting rid of their spiritual frustrations. And these teachers were subtly providing some hope. Like, if your sense of contraction turns into boundlessness, you will feel unconditional love and your spiritual search is over. And if you come to a five-day retreat, you are even more likely to lose your ego. But they suggest these things indirectly.

JK: I see.

Q: They say, "When you don't live in the past or future, everything will just be happening of its own accord. Then there will be no more resistance. Then there will be happiness without a cause." They can formulate their words more subtly than I can, but that is what some seem to communicate. They will deny this, of course. They are more eloquent than me.

JK: Right.

Q: If the person is not real, why would anyone be interested in a peaceful and happy life? My husband is always laughing at me when I went to one of those retreats, because he is very eloquent when it comes to expressing adverse or disapproving comments. He is a lawyer, you know. He encouraged me to be critical about this subject and the way some people present themselves as communicators or writers about this subject. But I believe he lacks the experience of the dropping away of personhood. He tries to understand with his head. Maybe he is a bit frustrated about that. He hates it when these teachers allow others to believe that they are experts in liberation. He believes they are arrogant, but I don't feel that way at all. I must say that the first time 'my' personhood dropped away – if I can use these terms – it was a huge experience. And I really saw there was nobody home. And yet, I feel that there is no need to claim anything because talking about it is exactly contradicting the message, isn't it? Mahatma Gandhi said, "Speak only if it improves upon the silence."

JK: I believe you are right in the sense that silence is better than words or concepts. On the other hand, I believe that when one has had such an experience, there may appear a desire to share this with others. Although there might also be frustration that this can't be conveyed properly in words. Maybe art, music and poetry are better tools, I don't know. But there is a pleasure in sharing this, especially when a resonance is felt between the communicator and his or her audience. I believe a lot of people go to such meetings for that reason. They seem to love to be there. They have heard the message, they know all about it, and yet they go again. Some seekers – especially those who are strongly identified with their path - hate these teachers because they say there is nowhere to go and nothing can be done. Others, however, have less worries and less expectations in life after sitting there, it makes them feel better - then that is a bonus. If listening to such Advaita teachers makes them feel lighter and less frustrated, then that's fine.

Q: In the end, it doesn't matter whether they are talking from experience or belief.

JK: There is no need to check out the communicator. He or she is only a small plastic Wi-Fi loudspeaker. Don't spend your time in examining the finger pointing to the moon. Don't shoot the messenger. Then you are focusing on the personal level. You are looking for labels. You are focusing on the personal realm and not on the universal. I am not suggesting you should stop criticizing these teachers, and I am not saying that you should believe whatever they say. I just feel it isn't so important. Remember that I wrote that there are three major tools the ego uses to survive: the division between me and others, between past and future, and between high and low. Checking out if one teacher is better than another one, for example, is a nice example of both focusing on the personal and on labeling. No need to go there, it is a mental battlefield. I prefer to point to that which is impersonal and cannot be labeled.

In nondualism, there are
no enlightened masters
and no unenlightened pupils.
That very distinction, that labelling
would be another form of dualism.

It is Unattainable

Q: You sometimes say that recognizing what you already are is better than any practice. You said, "Just be. It takes no effort."

JK: I don't need to order you to do this as a kind of technique, simply recognize it's already the case anyway. The tiger doesn't need a seven steps program or a three-year spiritual course to be what she already is. Even when the tiger wears the mask of a cat, she's still a tiger. I just point out that you are a beautiful tiger wearing a mask of a cat. And you believe you are a cat because you have a cat's name, and you learned to behave like one. And then you are reading books on how to become a tiger.

Q: Nothing to do, and yet something is recognized. That still sounds like a process while you said there is no process. And taking of that mask might take some effort, otherwise I would have done it years ago. So, it seems that a little effort is necessary.

JK: It is a paradox. I use words to point to the wordless. It seems to take time to be timeless. It looks as if the seeker needs a body to see that you are not limited to this body. But the tiger is not about you. That is the down side of this analogy. Don't put on a mask of a tiger now! The tiger is not a bigger spiritual ego, it stands for the impersonal space. The cat stands for the ego, the tiger stands for egolessness.

Q: I see.

JK: But don't let your mind try and analyse this. No need to evaluate your own state, no need to compare yourself with others, no need to put yourself under a test, no need to expect a special personal state. If you don't feed the mind with old or new tricks, your mind might get quiet. This looks like a silent natural state but it's not a state you can come in and go out, it's the spaciousness which allows all sorts of states. You can be busy with your work and with plenty of social activities, and yet the silence is here. This space is never away, like the physical space we have here in this room. This space was already here before we came in, it is here right now, and this space won't leave the room when we leave the room. We might think that this space is limited by the floor, the four walls and the ceiling, just as we think that our awareness is limited to the borders made by the skin surrounding our body. But the space doesn't stop at these walls, it goes into all directions and has no borders.

Q: It's bigger than the universe.

JK: And it can't age. After thousands of years this space hasn't grown old. It didn't become a smaller space or a space of a lower quality. And the space in the room is the same quality as the space outside the room, on the street, in the park, in the whole neighborhood and beyond. The spaciousness in your body and the spaciousness in 'my' body are exactly the same. It is universal, egoless and singular. It is secretive and ordinary at the same time. Nobody is excluded. It's a common aliveness or isness. It's the wetness of the ocean.

Q: I know I am this but I can't attain it.

JK: It is unattainable. Just *be*, no mind is necessary. No philosophical wisdom can close the deal. No emotional release is needed to be aware of awareness. No need to create, think, visualize, imagine or expect something. No need for trying or going elsewhere. How you feel, where you are, it can't influence the awareness of just being. Don't look for an answer. Don't try to explain. Don't expect you can say, "I got it". Don't look for any confirmation from yourself or from an outsider, because that would only be a confirmation of a special state or of an experience of the seeker you believe you are. The cat looks for confirmation all the time, but the tiger – the space underneath the mask - doesn't need any confirmation because it is already everything. The neutral seer cannot be seen, it can only be. The spaciousness cannot be moved aside, that attempt would also appear in and as the same spaciousness. You can't aim for it. It's not a task because we are all already beingness. We are not separate from is-ness. Seeing *this* is a 'zero second meditation', because it takes no time. Feeling *this* is a 'zero-centimetre meditation', because it takes no distance. It's also a 'zero-person meditation', as the person isn't invited in this meditation.

Q: This meditation points immediately to the source.

JK: Yes, it is immediate, timeless. But it has no source, it has no centre. It is sometimes symbolized by zero. When children learn to count, they start by 1, and then go to two, three and so on. In nondualism we start at zero. You start as a new-born baby as zero, we are all 0. It is the sense of naked being. The me is 1. Your mother is 2. Your father 3. Your sister 4. A common advice in nondualism is that you stay in and as zero, until the efforts to stay in and as 0 disappear. But then I must add the question, who would stay in zero? Anyway, whether you have thoughts or no thoughts, does it affect the zero? Can certain thoughts or actions stain the zero? Can certain actors damage the white canvas of the cinema?

Q: My master said that both understanding and devotion are needed. I believe I have the full understanding, but I am not so sure about my devotional qualities. Is it necessary that the mind becomes silent and that the heart opens, before one can say that the spiritual search has ended? Wouldn't that concept be another very subtle condition on that space which doesn't know any conditions?

JK: To use your words, the so-called opening of the heart is very likely to happen when the sense of personhood is unmasked, but it is not a condition. Unconditional love is more likely to be felt when there is no ego involved. But you don't have to hug everybody on the street now. And that sense of love might not be permanent. And then you may complain you lost it again when you feel angry or frustrated. It all still sounds personal to me. It might be a result of the insights you received, and that may be very spectacular - if before that experience your heart was (apparently) closed. But let's not go into such stories too much. And the heart we refer to in nondualism is not capable of opening and closing.

Q: But it seems to me that my master has achieved an opening of his heart permanently. We should all be in this space continuously, isn't it?

JK: Are you talking about the real space or are you referring to a personal achievement of a spiritual master? It is important to be vigilant here. Is your spiritual ego aiming at some state of inner silence or openness of the heart which the master has achieved and which you haven't attained yet? If this would be the case, notice that there is no need to chase that state. It is the spiritual ego who wants to reach that. When there is clarity, this subtle spiritual game is unmasked - without any need for criticism on the master and his followers.

This subtle game is rather observed with a compassionate smile because this story of master and devotees is also a play of consciousness. The inner voice which says that things are as they are, or the voice which says that things should be different, these are only sounds passing by. The voice which whispers there should be no more 1 but only zero, that voice is only an inner sound of less than a second and it doesn't deserve more attention than the next sound. If it appears, it appears. And if it doesn't appear, it simply doesn't appear. Clouds come and go. No need to complain about the weather, and if complaining about grey clouds and rain arises, that's not a problem either. And if complaining is considered as a problem, that's also what's arising. Words fail to describe the what is. The 'what is' doesn't need a master to say that there is only 'the what is and nothing else.' No need to confirm to yourself or to others that you are *in* and *as* the 'what is,' or that you melted away in the is-ness, or that egocentric voices don't appear any more in your movie, or that your heart is always open. All that usually disappears. And if it's still appearing, that is not a problem either.

Q: You simply keep quiet and live from the silence and love from your heart.

JK: That sounds good, but it might be another advice which is addressing the seeker, who might reach a better state in the future, while nondualism tries to point to what all beings have in common, even those who are generally considered to be the bad guys.

Q: So, there shouldn't be a "this shouldn't be"?

JK: Even that is not necessary.

Nondualism is not designed
to solve your problems.
It might invite the reader
to check who owns those problems.

Both Real and Unreal

Q: Some teachers of Advaita say that there is no separate person and therefore no free will. Does it imply that it is only a matter of grace or good luck whether the sense of ego drops away at some point during the quest?

JK: Such questions obviously originate from the seeking mind. And any answer to such a question will most likely frustrate that same mind. The sense of ego doesn't just drop away, it *was* never a solid thing or entity in the first place.
The voices of the seeker try to find a solution to something which can't be solved with the mind. It is as if I would give you a delicious tomato soup, I know you love it and I know you are very hungry, and yet I tell you that you must eat it with a fork.

Q: On the other hand, it can be a sudden or a gradual event in the story to unmask the voices which suggest that the seeker is real.

JK: But the paradox is that the seeker can't unmask these voices.

Q: At some point, I gave up all the seeking. I felt as if I had gone all the way, without any results. I even stopped trying to solve the problem. I couldn't find any spoon to eat my tomato soup, and realized there are no spoons available. I gave up. The urge or the habit to meditate also melted away. At the same time, I never intended to stop meditating. And there was a sense of total surrender, of relief. I went from the path of Jnana yoga, the path of mental discrimination, to the path of Bhakti, the path of devotion. The path of the heart. But I didn't surrender to a master or holy historical figure like Buddha or Jesus, I just surrendered.

JK: There can indeed be a surrender to what is present. It could be to a person or an object or an idea or a feeling. You can surrender to the sun or the moon, to a mountain or the stars, to a piece of art, to the body of your lover, to the picture of a holy saint, it doesn't matter. But the danger is that one gets distracted by the object of surrender. No need to put your tent at that object of surrender. In nondualism, we would rather say it is a surrender to *presence.* An impersonal devotion to the 'what is.' And the 'what is' can be a candle, your breathing, a cloud passing by, pain in your neck, just anything. We could call it surrender to life as it is.

Q: Just surrendering to the 'what is.'

JK: But there is no seeker doing or planning such surrender, because the latter would be the outcome of an agenda, the result of a strategy. It is like a child who surrenders to playing with sand on the beach, it is very simple and ordinary. Just a devotion to the simplicity of the moment, without any need for expectations or regrets. Just being without labelling. And life just flows. Time is said to be an illusion, and yet there seems to be time when we look at a clock. It is like a surrender to the river of life which seems to stream in a certain way. Just surrender to what is, and the magic is that nobody can do it. It is like pouring water into water, it is like pouring oil into oil, it is simple and magical at the same time. And this 'what is' is both everything and yet, it is also nothing. It is *everything* because it doesn't have any borders, and it is *nothing* because it can't be grasped, described or possessed.

If you still feel you have to stay
in a peaceful state of mind
without interruption,
you are still striving for something.
You are still focusing on the me.
Nondualism tries to point to the I,
the impersonal beingness.
This limitless I doesn't know
about effort or continuity.

An Awakening Event

Q: Several teachers I have come across, describe an event which was like a glimpse of pure beingness. Some of them also suggest that this was a milestone in their spiritual search. Some even use the words 'before' and 'after' that event. Others say it doesn't matter so much. What are your thoughts on this?

JK: The realization of the impersonal nature of what we truly are may come before such an event, during a glimpse or afterwards. Or even without any glimpse at all! There are no rules. Beingness is all-embracing and therefore excludes nothing or nobody. No need to give a lot of attention to such stories. The major down side of reading or hearing about such stories is that they set up an expectation that something special needs to occur to give yourself the permission to have recognized *experientially* what you really are. You can only experience the falling away of the old mask, but you can't experience the original face, as Buddhists describe it. We might say that the mask becomes more transparent, more translucent. But even that is only an image, of course.

I also want to add here that all these stories fall apart as soon as it is clear that time is a concept. The belief in time is one of the three major tools of the spiritual ego. The recognition of what we really are is not something the seeker can achieve by following an evolutionary path because such a spiritual path suggests an evolution over time. Beingness doesn't *know* what past or future is. It even doesn't know what the present moment means. It couldn't care less.

Q: In other words, any expectation a spiritual seeker might have about finding the ultimate truth is a sign of not being clear enough?

JK: Any technique which is future-oriented, is doomed to be misleading. And yet, even these 'misleading' techniques which have a higher goal in mind, are also part of that which is. And to whom would these techniques be misleading? No need to worry about people following progressive paths. No need to criticize masters who promote progressive paths. Progressive paths are also an expression of the one aware beingness. It is just what is. If it *is*, it is. If it is not, it is not. That's how simple this nondual philosophy is. And nobody can argue with that which is. Because it is.

Q: If there is no individual who can chose or decide, does this mean that all is already planned?

JK: You are pointing to the personal level again. For a person, such a question is important. For beingness, it means nothing. There is just the everchanging play of consciousness. There is just the never-ending stream of pure awareness. It is full and empty at the same time. It is like you put your

256

hand in a mountain river, and you feel the cold water gliding through your fingers. You hear the sounds of the water, you sense the cool freshness of the passing water. And yet, you can't grasp it. You can't take it home to show your friends. You can't possess the river by closing your hand. You might take a photograph of the river with your smartphone and put it on Facebook, but that will only be a two-dimensional picture – not the real thing. You might try to fill your hand with a handful of water, but then you will miss the natural flow and freshness of the mountain river. You might take a video of your hand in the flowing water and put it on Instagram, but the video will not cover the freshness of the 'real' experience. This is ungraspable, unknowable, unattainable.

Q: Some teachers say that oneness or beingness wants to have the experience of being limited. For that reason, it has created time and personhood and causality. Oneness plays hide and seek with itself. What are your thoughts on this?

JK: I have no idea how or why all this happens. I have no story like the one you mentioned. It sounds good, but it is only a story. It may please some people, but I am not finding it very interesting. I believe the 'one and only' has no desire to play the game of hide and seek, because there is nobody else. It doesn't need to pretend anything. It is.

Q: So, there is no higher goal either?

JK: All I can say is that life happens, and that is a miracle to 'me.' It is a childlike sense of wonder. This is-ness is a miracle. I don't feel any need to add a nice story to this. I don't think that oneness has any need or desire to express itself on whatever level. If one is infinite, there is only the infinite. There can't be any desire or need. Such a story is just a projection of our human mind onto the infinite.

Q: Once this is clear, there is no need to project anything at all onto the infinite. Even not a creator who has created the is-ness. Seekers can have such needs, apparently, but the beingness doesn't need anything because it lacks nothing.

JK: It is everything already. But our minds are too small to get this. My mind can't get this either.

Q: Why do I feel so much lighter and more loving during a glimpse into pure is-ness?

JK: During a glimpse, nothing is added, but it can feel peaceful because 'you' enjoy the absence of mental trouble. It can feel blissful because the inner voices are still. There are no expectations, no regrets, no labelling of yourself, no labelling of others. The absence of labelling may also give a deep sense of unconditional love. But you can't claim this condition as a state. In fact, you were totally 'absent' as a separate person during the glimpse, but your voices claim *you* experienced it.

Q: I was absent when my 'me' imploded?

JK: It is a bit like someone sticks a needle in your balloon, and you explode with a bang. Only to realize that the air inside and outside are the same. But if you want to experience another 'bang', another glimpse, you need to blow up your ego balloon again. And write your name on it. Until someone sticks a needle in it again. Why not? It looks like a game, but it's only play.

Q: Instead of a bang, it can also be gentle, like the silence from within is whispering to you.

JK: Yes, it doesn't have to be a sudden 'bang'.

Q: It may go slowly, although this sounds like a process again.

JK: Suppose you are snorkelling, and you look down into the deep. Your ears are under the water level, so all the sounds of the chattering egos are gone, and that silence feels good, it feels like coming home. This vast spaciousness under the water feels familiar, more familiar than the ego who is swimming on the surface! And this deep blue is so peaceful because no other egos are swimming down there. And you can't hear their shouting voices.

There are no sharks in the deep. You realize that all the noise is on the surface. Your ego would like to go 'down' there, would like to build a nest in the deepest layers. It would like to reside as a person on the bottom of the ocean, but you are like a cork, your body always comes up to the surface immediately. The body stays on the surface, the wave can't dive in the deep.

Q: But I heard amazing stories of seekers who experienced peace and joy, and I also saw beautiful colours.

JK: You can fantasize that you're going down like a scuba diver into a magic world, and your mind can create the most amazing stories. The brain can create virtual experiences of the deep blue, but these are just tricks of the mind. The brain can create fantastic virtual realities, it is a master in hallucination and imagination. But that is also all play. And it is all fine. But it doesn't *improve* the awareness.

Q: Still I had my own nice experiences. The sense of peace and inner contentment were real, they were *not* a phantasy. They happened to *me*, not to my neighbour or so.

JK: Yes. It is a paradox. You have these glimpses while the ego is absent. And the voice of the ego tries to claim it afterwards. Just putting your ears under water is enough to notice the silence under the surface. Just looking down into the deep is enough to realise the peace underneath.

In this metaphor, I need to add that there is no swimmer on the surface looking down through swim goggles, it is the wave 'looking down' into the deep, recognizing its own wetness in the deep. It is the wave realizing it is also made of the same water at the surface as the water in the deepest layers.

There's nothing 'our me' can do
to rid ourselves of this parasite in our head,
because the separate 'me' is the parasite.

Other books by Dr. Jan Kersschot

Coming Home (Inspiration, Editions India), also in Spanish (Sirio)

Nobody Home (Watkins, New Age Books India, Non-Duality Press, New Harbinger) Also in Dutch (Ankh Hermes), German (J. Kamphausen), Spanish (Gulaab), Russian, Japanese (Natural Spirit)

This Is It (Watkins) Also in Spanish (Gulaab), Dutch (Ankh Hermes) and Korean

The Myth of Self-Inquiry (Non-Duality Press)

Biopuncture (Medical Textbooks available in English, Spanish, Russian, French, German)

Bodyscapes (Black and White Photography)

See also: www.kersschot.com

Who are we? What are we?
These questions have
no beginning and no end.
We cannot answer the questions,
we can only *be* the answer.

Printed in Great Britain
by Amazon

37987941R00152